# How To Grow
## The
# WILDFLOWERS

written by

Eric A. Johnson & Scott Millard

—

major photography by

Scott Millard, Michael Landis & Charles Mann

—

illustrations by

Don Fox

**Editing, Design & Production**

Millard Publishing Services, Tucson, Arizona

Editorial Assistant
Michele V. M. Millard

Proofreader
Mary Campbell Nielsen

Indexing
Byliner/Pat Hollinshead

Typesetting
The Service Bureau

Copyright© 1993
Millard Publishing Services and Eric A. Johnson Co.

All rights reserved. No part of this book may be reproduced or transmitted in any form or by any means, electronic or mechanical, including photocopy, without written permission from the publisher.
Printing 10 9 8 7 6 5 4 3 2

Printed in China
ISBN 0-9628236-2-7
Library of Congress Catalog Card Number 93-077365

Cover photo: A basket filled with mixed wildflowers. Photo by Michael Landis

Title page photo: *Lupinus* species photo by Scott Millard

The information in this book is true and accurate to the best of our knowledge. It is offered without guarantees on the part of the authors, who disclaim liability in connection with the use of this information.

Address inquiries to:
IRONWOOD PRESS
2968 West Ina Road #285
Tucson, Arizona  85741

**Photography**

Elizabeth Ball
44 top, 84 bottom, 85 bottom

Cathy Barash
69 bottom right

Thomas Eltzroth
85 top, 105 bottom right

Environmental Seed Producers
25 bottom, 49 top left, 57 top left, 57 top right, 65 top, 68 top left

Saxon Holt
48 bottom, 56 top, 61 top left, 73 top, 73 bottom left, 73 bottom right, 93 top left, 101 top

Michael Landis
pages 4, 13, 21, 31, 36, 40 top left, 44 bottom, 49 bottom left, 49 bottom right, 52 top, 57 bottom, 60 top left, 61 top right, 68 top right, 68 bottom, 76 top right, 76 bottom, 80 top, 81 top right, 81 bottom, 88 bottom right, 93 top right, 93 bottom right, 100 top, 100 bottom, 101 bottom, 104 top,

Charles Mann
pages 16, 17, 19, 27, 48 top left, 48 top right, 49 top right, 56 bottom, 64 top, 69 top, 80 bottom, 84 top, 88 top, 89 top, 93 bottom left, 96 bottom, 109 bottom

Scott Millard
pages 1, 4, 5, 8, 9, 12(2), 20, 22, 23(2), 24, 25 top, 26, 28(2), 29(2), 30, 32, 33, 37, 40 top right, 40 bottom, 45 top, 45 bottom, 52 bottom left, 52 bottom right, 52 bottom right, 60 top right, 60 bottom, 61 bottom, 64 bottom, 65 bottom, 69 bottom left, 76 top left, 81 top left, 88 bottom left, 89 bottom, 96 top left, 96 top right, 97 top, 97 bottom, 104 bottom, 105 top, 105 bottom left, 109 top left, 109 top right, 112

**For their patience and understanding, sincere thanks go to:**

Maxine Johnson, Palm Desert, CA

and

Michele V. M. Millard, Tucson, AZ

**For their assistance, thanks to:**

Charles Basham, consultant, Huntington Harbor, CA

Martha Blane, seed consultant, San Marcos, CA

Jack Bodger, Environmental Seed Producers, Lompoc, CA

Dennis Bryson, Theodore Payne Foundation, Sun Valley, CA

Janice Busco, Theodore Payne Foundation, Sun Valley, CA

Mark Dimmitt, botanist, Arizona-Sonora Desert Museum, Tucson, AZ

Cliff Douglas, Arid Zone Trees, Queen Creek, AZ

Chris Drayer, Landscape Architect, San Diego, CA

Peter Duncombe, Desert Demonstration Garden, Las Vegas, NV

Ron Gass, Mountain States Nursery, Phoenix, AZ

John Harlow Jr., Harlow's Nursery, Tucson, AZ

Michael MacCaskey, *National Gardening* magazine, Burlington, VT

Steve Martino, Landscape Architect, Phoenix, AZ

Gary Maskarinec, Wildseed, Tempe, AZ

Judy Mielke, horticulturist, Tempe, AZ

Bette Nesbitt, horticulturist, Tucson, AZ

Robert Perry, Landscape Architect, LaVerne, CA

S&S Seed Co., Carpenteria, CA

Victor Schaff, seedsman, Carpenteria, CA

Kirk Schneider, irrigation consultant, Vista, CA

W.G. Scotty Scott, landscape consultant, La Quinta, CA

Ken Smith, Landscape Architect, Newberry Park, CA

John Stewart, Living Desert, Palm Desert, CA

Dennis Swartzell, horticulturist, UNLV Arboretum, NV

Lance Walheim, horticultural consultant, Exeter, CA

Sally Wasowski, Landscape Architect, Dallas, TX

Jim Wheat, Landscape Architect, Tempe, AZ

**Additional thanks goes to the botanical gardens and arboretums where many plants and garden scenes in this book were photographed.**

Descanso Gardens, La Canada, CA

Desert Botanical Garden, Phoenix, AZ

Landscapes Southern California Style, Riverside, CA

Los Angeles State & County Arboretum, Arcadia, CA

Rancho Santa Ana Botanic Garden, Claremont, CA

Santa Barbara Botanic Garden, Santa Barbara, CA

South Coast Botanic Garden, Palos Verdes Peninsula, CA

Tohono Chul Park, Tucson, AZ

Tucson Botanical Gardens, Tucson, AZ

# Table of Contents

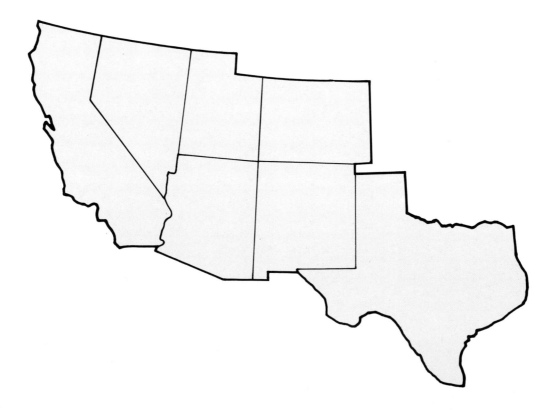

# WILDFLOWER GARDENING IN THE WEST

Wildflowers have long been admired for the beauty they bring to nature. Particularly in the West, residents and visitors alike eagerly anticipate the annual springtime show. We've come to *know* the wildflowers in the natural environment, but their potential as flowering plants around home landscapes has largely gone untapped. And that is what this book is about: learning *how to grow the wildflowers* and how to enjoy them around our homes.

## Time-Honored Plants, New Opportunities

Wildflowers present gardeners and homeowners with opportunities to shift away from labor-intensive landscapes of lawn and trimmed hedges. With proper site preparation, wildflowers require much less maintenance and water than traditional garden plants. Wildflowers, for example, can replace all or part of a thirsty lawn. Or you can grow them during the spring and early summer instead of high-water-use bedding plants. After annual wildflowers have completed their bloom period, the planting area can be left fallow, requiring no water or care except for occasional weeding and raking. With time many wildflowers naturalize, reseeding so new plants emerge each season.

A small caution is in order: Wildflower gardening is not the simple task of scattering seeds from a can or packet, to be forgotten until they break into furious bloom. The emphasis in this book (and one of the keys to success) is proper preparation before you plant. The basic instructions on how to plan a wildflower garden and install it properly are provided in these pages.

Aside from their natural beauty, there's an even simpler role that wildflowers play in our lives: fulfilling the urge to plant something and watch it grow. For most gardeners, it doesn't matter if their garden is an acre-size meadow or a few containers on the patio. Sowing your own seeds and watching them evolve from tiny seedlings to mature plants that burst into full flower bring a reward unlike any other gardening activity.

A flowing carpet of *Oenethera belandieri*, Mexican evening primrose, greets visitors to this home in Tucson. Design: Margaret West.

Above: A planting of *Eschscholzia mexicana*, Mexican gold poppy, captures the interest and wonder of a young admirer.

## Wildflowers in the Natural Garden

A *natural garden* takes its cue from nature. Designs are informal without straight lines or adherence to symmetry. Plants, for the most part, are left unpruned and allowed to develop their natural character, much as they would in their native habitats. When a garden is composed of native plants, it takes on the unique identity of the region and the community. When given time to mature, these landscapes evolve to create a diverse, natural environment. They encourage soil and water conservation and provide back-yard refuges well suited as wild-life habitats. A natural garden also relies on a balanced approach to pest and disease control, avoiding use of chemical sprays. The diversity of plants creates a self-sustaining environment of food, cover and shelter for insects, butterflies, birds and animals.

A natural garden design is guided by the seasons and the will of plants to grow, flower and set seed, rather than weekly control by lawn mower and hedge clippers. To put it another way, your participation as gardener-caretaker is one of gentle persuasion rather than power-tool domination. A natural garden can actually be more difficult to create than a conventional scene of lawn, bedding plants, foundation shrubs and trees. In fact, a natural garden design may not be for everyone. Some may not enjoy the casual, seemingly haphazard appearance, feeling more comfortable in controlled surroundings.

But it is not necessary to totally abandon a traditional landscape for a natural garden design. A natural garden can be blended into existing landscapes, and this is often the best way to begin. Mixed borders, described on page 27, and wildflower meadows, pages 27 to 28, are forms of natural gardens.

Wildflowers in a natural garden design provide new, sensible, environmentally sound choices. They also help reduce water use by the very nature of their life cycle. In the arid West, where water is a precious resource, a natural garden philosophy is right at home. The water-efficient designs and gardening practices show us common-sense ways to beautify our surroundings.

## Common-Sense Conservation

Human beings can have a profound impact on our surroundings. Unintentionally (or even intentionally), our actions can reduce our quality of life, as well as the future quality of life of our children. Wildflower gardeners and visitors to natural wildflower preserves can bring about positive changes to help ensure the preservation of native plants and increase awareness of the value they bring to all of us.

When you visit natural wildflower preserves, avoid the temptation to collect flowers, plants or seeds. The isolated action of picking a few flowers may not amount to much, but consider what would occur if every visitor picked only a few. In some instances the plants could be rare at that location and all seeds should remain on site so the plant will remain established there. By removing the flowers the seeds are removed, and the plant has lost its ability to reproduce. Many state laws also prohibit collection of plants in the wild and carry stiff penalties for abuse.

When visiting natural areas that feature wildflowers, remain on paths and drive only on established roads. Indiscriminate trampling can cause more damage than picking flowers or collecting seeds. The same is true if you are taking photographs. In other words, leave the area as you found it.

When purchasing plants and seeds, buy only from reputable companies. Purchase plants that the supplier has propagated. Purchasing plants that have been collected in the wild depletes their ability to remain established. If you're not sure how the plant was propagated or if it is priced suspiciously low, ask the supplier about the source. If you're not comfortable with the answer, look elsewhere.

To learn more about the native plants in your area, contact the native plant society office in your state or the nearest botanical garden. Each offers education in the form of literature, tours and classes on native plants.

# Introduction to Dry Climates

Sunshine, seasonal temperatures (both high and low), rainfall (timing and amounts), wind, soil and other elements help create the gardening conditions in your own backyard. Understanding these factors, common to every climate, helps you recognize and take advantage of your own garden's unique growing conditions. In other words, when you become a *climate-wise gardener,* you garden with nature instead of against it, planting and caring for adapted plants according to the progression of the seasons.

## The Sun

The amount of sunshine your garden receives depends on several factors. These include light intensity during the seasons; the direction of exposure (going from highest to lowest: south, west, east, north) and the amount of shade from plants and structures. Extreme sunshine and heat can kill plants or adversely affect their growth. High temperatures, intense sunlight and inadequate water stress plants, causing them to produce fewer flowers for a shorter period of time. This is particularly true of plants introduced to hot arid regions from more temperate climates. They are even more likely to fail if they're located in southern or western exposures where sunlight and high temperatures are most intense.

Temperatures higher than 90F take a toll on newly planted plants as well as those unadapted to heat. Signs of high-temperature damage are browning at edges and tips of mature leaves and wilting of new growth. Plants in fast-draining, sandy soils are highly susceptible to heat damage because water drains rapidly away from the root zone. High temperatures can also increase the temperature of the upper layer of soil to the extent that roots near the soil surface are killed. Shallow-rooted annuals and perennials are particularly susceptible.

In coastal gardens, *not enough* sunshine and heat can be a problem. Conditions are often too cool, cloudy and foggy for plants that require heat to produce flowers. If you live along the coast, select plants adapted to these conditions, and locate plants in the sunniest locations in your garden—south and west exposures. Reflected heat and light from light-colored walls also raise temperatures.

## Cold Temperatures

Every plant has a low-temperature tolerance. *Annual* plants are programmed to flower, set seed and die with the first fall frost. *Perennial* plants live year after year, but can be damaged when the temperature drops below the plants' inherent tolerance point. How long cold temperatures last and how quickly they drop affect the extent of the damage. The faster the drop, the worse the injury. Cold that lasts for an hour or less may not hurt plants, but if it stays cold for the whole evening, severe damage is likely. If the cold is severe or prolonged, the plant could be killed.

If the plant is under stress due to lack of moisture, or if it has recently been planted, it is more susceptible to cold injury. The time of year matters as well. When cold temperatures occur late in spring shortly after plants have produced new, tender growth, the damage will be more severe than if the new growth had an opportunity to gradually adjust to cooler temperatures.

## Rainfall

With the exceptions of the northern California coast and higher-elevation regions, the West does not receive abundant rainfall, although rainfall can fluctuate greatly from year to year. Yuma, Arizona, for example, has recorded annual rainfall ranging from less than 1 inch to over 11 inches.

Mountain ranges in the West help determine where rain is distributed. Warm, moist air rises and cools rapidly when it comes in contact with abrupt changes in elevation. The result is condensation and rainfall. After the moisture has been "wrung" from the clouds, there is often little remaining for areas beyond. This is called the *rain shadow effect.* A large-scale example exists in Nevada, where the Sierra Nevada Mountains stand in the way of coastal storms carrying moisture-laden air. Similarly, the San Jacinto Mountains block rains from reaching the Coachella Valley.

Throughout much of California, a *Mediterranean* climate prevails, with rainfall coming during winter and spring followed by a warm, dry

The extent and timing of rainfall is largely responsible for annual shows of wildflowers in natural settings. In general, when rains are early followed by warm, sunny weather, wildflowers bloom ahead of schedule. But early rains followed by warm weather tends to cause them to set seed early, shortening the bloom period. When rains occur later and are followed by cool, cloudy weather, the flowering season will be later in spring, but it will last for a longer period.

summer and fall. The lowlands along the coast from Santa Barbara to San Diego are typical. Other regions of the world with this type of climate include South Africa, Chile, western Australia and the Mediterranean.

Winter rains are one reason why many wildflowers are planted in the fall—so they can benefit from the moist soil conditions and moderate temperatures. Many native California plants and natives of similar Mediterranean climates also have natural adaptations that cause them to become dormant or semi-dormant during the warm, rainless summers. Because of these adaptations, many native plants may not tolerate regular summer water in a home garden. (An exception is newly planted plants; they should receive regular water until established.)

## Humidity

How does humidity affect gardening and water needs of plants? In a low-humidity climate, the rate of evaporation from plants and the soil surface can be quite rapid. Low humidity also causes rainfall to evaporate rapidly, to the extent that little actually accumulates in the soil. Low humidity, in combination with hot, dry winds, high temperatures and intense sunlight, causes plants to dry out very quickly. During these conditions, pay close

attention to the appearance of your plants. Consider using the hydro-zoning principle discussed on page 24. Placing plants in groups helps increase humidity around them, reducing moisture need.

## Wind

Many areas of the West experience high winds—often in spring, occasionally in fall. In much of Southern California, Santa Ana winds sweep through mountain passes into San Bernardino, Riverside, the San Fernando Valley, and Ventura and Orange counties. In California's Coachella Valley and in high desert areas, winds up to 40 or more miles per hour are common. Las Vegas experiences strong winds throughout the year, especially in spring.

Windstorms can turn into sandstorms in many of these areas. Sand blown at a high velocity can seriously damage plants. In some instances the wind-blown sand builds up in watering basins and landscaped areas. Planting living windbreaks and providing protection such as fences or walls, especially for newly planted plants, are necessary in wind-prone regions. Wind, when accompanied by high temperatures, also dries plants out rapidly, causing them to require considerably more water.

## Garden Climates in the Arid West

Climates in the West range from the extreme cold of high elevation, mountainous regions such as those in and around the Rocky Mountains and Sierra Nevada, to moderate coastal climates to the hot, arid Chihuahuan, Sonoran and Mojave Deserts of the Southwest. This book focuses on the dry regions where low rainfall, high temperatures, low humidity and other factors prevent moisture from accummulating in the soil.

The following pages describe the climates of Arizona, California, Colorado, Nevada, New Mexico, Utah and Texas. Most states are subdivided further to account for major geographic conditions. For example, Southern California has four major climate zones: *Coastal, Inland Valleys, Low Deserts* and *Medium and High Deserts*. Likewise, in Texas, four

zones within the drier, western portion of the state are discussed—from San Antonio west to El Paso. Regions covered include the *Texas High Plains, Edwards Plateau, Red Rolling Plains* and the *Trans-Pecos Region*.

To see firsthand how climate determines which plants can grow in a region, visit botanical gardens and arboretums. Compare, for example, botanical gardens in Southern California. Tropical plants thrive in coastal gardens such as Quail Botanical Gardens in Encinitas. Less than 40 miles inland, at Rancho Santa Ana in Claremont, colder temperatures and lack of ocean influence require that more cold-hardy plants be grown. The contrast is even more dramatic in nearby desert regions. The plant palette at the Living Desert in Palm Desert includes many cacti and flowering desert plants that have adapted to survive in extremely hot, arid conditions.

Public arboretums and demonstration gardens are excellent sources of information on wildflowers. A listing of public gardens in the arid western states is provided on page 125. Shown above is Landscapes Southern California Style, a demonstration garden sponsored by the Western Municipal Water District in Riverside, California.

| | |
|---|---|
| Barstow | 4.50 |
| Blythe | 4.10 |
| Brawley | 2.45 |
| Claremont | 18.05 |
| Escondido | 17.10 |
| Los Angeles | 14.75 |
| Needles | 4.60 |
| Palm Springs | 3.70 |
| Pasadena | 20.00 |
| Riverside | 11.05 |
| San Bernardino | 16.85 |
| San Diego | 10.10 |
| Tustin (near) | 12.65 |
| Santa Barbara | 18.90 |
| Ventura | 15.30 |

Source: *Climate and Man*

# Southern California

In this book, the climates of Southern California are organized into four basic climate zones: *Coastal, Inland Valleys, Low Desert* and *Medium and High Deserts.* The following provides an overview; climates here are quite complex. For more specific information on your local climate, contact your state or county cooperative extension service, or consult an experienced nurseryman or Master Gardener in your neighborhood.

**Southern California Coast—**
This is the region along the Pacific Coast that includes cities from Santa Barbara in the north to San Diego in the south. The Pacific Ocean rules this climate, and winds and fog are common. An exception occurs when hot Santa Ana winds blow in from nearby deserts, increasing temperatures and drying out plants. Summer sunshine and temperatures are moderate, and humidity is high compared to inland regions, which means plants need less water. Low temperatures are normally quite mild, and tropical and sub-tropical plants are commonly grown outdoors year-round. Seasonal and day-to-day temperature ranges are small, the opposite of desert regions.

Thermal belts exist near the coast where temperatures are mild but the additional heat allows plants such as avocado to thrive. This is the climate of Camarillo, Beverly Hills, Whittier, Fullerton and Vista.

In the greater Los Angeles area, cold air flows down from hillsides to gather in low valleys below the thermal belts. This reduces the amount of heat available to plants and makes winter lows even lower. Even so, normal winter low temperatures rarely drop below 28F. In summer, morning fog creeps inland as far as Pasadena and Whittier to lower temperatures and increase moisture, usually burning off the same afternoon. This is the climate of Torrance, Inglewood, Lakewood, Gardena and Irvine.

The *growing season,* days between the last and first frosts, is practically year-round, from 330 to 365 days. Generally, as you move inland, the growing season shortens. Rainfall averages range from 10 inches a year in San Diego to 18.90 inches at Santa Barbara.

Problem soils sometimes exist along the coast in the form of heavy clay with a calcareous base. Improving these soils with organic amendments helps increase drainage and workability. See page 114.

In this moderate, forgiving climate, planting can be done year-round. Summer plantings do require closer attention to moisture needs until plants are established.

**Southern California Inland—**
This large climate zone is composed of several smaller zones, including the coastal valleys and coastal plains, coastal and interior foothills and the warm thermal belts within. It is a region greatly affected by mountain ranges and local topography. In the northern stretches of Southern California are the *Transverse* ranges, which generally run east and west. In Orange, Riverside and San Diego Counties, the *Peninsular* ranges run north and south. The result is a jigsaw puzzle of diverse climates that are separated, in some instances, by only a few miles.

The nature of climate in inland Southern California largely depends on which imparts the greatest influence—the cool ocean or the hot, inland deserts. In some instances, both may, on a given day, literally depending on which way the wind is blowing.

Winter temperatures are lower inland than on the coast, which means gardeners must be more selective in where they locate tropical and sub-tropical plants. High temperatures are also higher by comparison—90F to 100F days in summer are common. This, along with the lower humidity, causes plants to demand more moisture. Higher temperatures allow plants that require heat to be grown here where they might fail along the coast. These include flowering plants native to desert regions such as red salvia, *Salvia greggii,* cassia, *Cassia* species, Texas ranger, *Leucophyllum* species and verbena, *Verbena* species.

Rainfall is most prevalent during winter and spring. These are annual averages for selected cities: Riverside, 11.05 inches; Pasadena, 20 inches and Claremont, 18.05 inches.

Escondido, Thousand Oaks, Pasadena, Whittier and Covina are in thermal belts that are regularly involved in a climactic tug of war between the influences of the cool coast and warm inland region. However, winters are generally mild, with normal low temperatures dropping to 36F to 23F, so cold-tender plants can often be grown successfully.

A similar but somewhat cooler climate is found in El Monte, Arcadia and Burbank. In the same situation as along the coast, cold air tends to gather in low valleys draining down from thermal belts, which further reduces winter lows. In this instance, normal winter low temperatures are 28F to 23F.

Areas of Southern California that are beyond the influence of the coast are affected by the local terrain and inland deserts. Thermal belts in these regions are generally 10F warmer in winter than the low, cool valleys below them. High heat—100F and above—is common. These warmer regions include Chatsworth in the west San Fernando Valley, San Bernardino, Riverside, Moreno Valley and Corona. Nearby cities that are not in warm thermal belts and have a slightly cooler climate include Woodland Hills, Pomona and Ontario.

Sow seed of wildflowers in fall to take advantage of winter rains. Plant hardy perennials and other hardy landscape plants in fall to early winter. After last spring frost, set out cold-tender annuals and perennials. Last spring frosts for this area include: Pasadena, February 3; San Bernardino, March 15; Santa Ana, February 7; Riverside, March 6.

**Southern California Low Deserts—** This is the climate of Palm Springs, Palm Desert, Brawley, Blythe and Indio. Conditions are similar to those in the low, subtropical desert of Arizona, described on page 14. However, summertime temperatures are typically hotter, and rainfall is even more scarce—a scant 4 to 5 inches a year, often even less.

In the Coachella, Imperial and Borrego Valleys, temperatures reach 110F to 115F in summer (sometimes more) and 26F to 32F in winter. Day-to-night temperature fluctuations can be considerable. In the lower Colorado River basin, temperature swings from the low 60sF to 110F can occur, a difference of almost 50F.

The Colorado River influences a long stretch from Laughlin, Nevada, through Needles, Blythe, Lake Havasu and Parker to Yuma, Arizona. The conditions are hot, dry and humid, with daily and seasonal temperatures similar to those in the Coachella Valley. The rugged terrain accounts for variable wind patterns that are often strong. Rainfall can be erratic, from very little to a lot. Summer rains are sometimes so heavy that highways are closed in wash areas.

Soil type plays an important role in watering and garden care. The sandy and alluvial soils that are so prevalent require that irrigations be more frequent than in loamy or clay-type soils, particularly for newly planted plants. Drip irrigation is commonly used when the design allows.

Fall planting is the rule for seeds as well as container plants. Plants become established before the high heat of summer. The growing season throughout the low deserts is a long 325 to 350 days, with average last spring frosts occurring in mid-January. In most years, less than a half-dozen evenings drop below freezing.

**Southern California Medium and High Deserts—** This is the climate of Lancaster, Palmdale, Hesperia, 29 Palms, Yucca Valley and Victorville. The medium desert generally includes areas within an elevation range of 1,000 to 7,000 feet, but it is commonly referred to as the "high desert." Climate here is largely affected by the elevation and terrain, and whether your landscape is in the path of cold-air drainage. Climate also depends on which exerts the greatest influence: the cold-winter mountain climates to the north or the hot, dry subtropical desert regions to the south and west. Valley floors are colder and the growing season is shorter compared to the warm thermal belts on slopes above them.

Summer temperatures are hot, well into the 100sF, but do not reach the plant-wilting highs or occur as frequently as in low-desert regions. Day-to-night and season-to-season temperature variations are almost as extreme as in the lower deserts. At elevations of 1,000 to 2,200 feet, normal winter lows are 20F to 22F; at 2,300 to 3,500 feet, lows range from 15F to 20F, although extremes are infrequently much lower. This climate has enough days below freezing to provide a definite winter season.

Winds are almost constant, blowing 10 to 20 mph most days. Strong winds 40 to 70 mph occur through the winter and spring months, particularly in areas away from sheltering mountains. Homes and plants greatly benefit from windbreaks and shelterbelts.

Over half this region receives less than 5 inches of rain each year, with some exceptions. Lancaster receives slightly more. If rains are plentiful in fall and winter as in most regions in the arid West, there's a good chance of seeing spring shows of wildflowers.

Plant cold-hardy plants in fall so they'll become established during the cool part of the year. Sow wildflower seed in fall as well. Wait until after last spring frost before planting tender perennials and annuals. Late frosts are common. Be prepared to protect newly planted plants in spring. Examples of average last spring frost dates are: Barstow, March 8; and Lancaster, March 31.

A wildflower meadow at Rancho Santa Ana in Claremont, California, features yellow *Limnanthes douglasii,* meadow foam, which thrives in wet locations.

Below, in Palm Desert, California, *Abronia villosa,* sand verbena, is well-adapted to the fast-draining sandy soils common to the region.

## Northern California Climates

**Northern California Coast and Coast Ranges**—The climate of this region, which extends from Santa Maria north, is governed by the ocean. This area is an extremely complex collection of climates, particularly around the San Francisco Bay Area. The following presents an overview. Contact local experts in your region for more complete information.

High temperatures along the coast during summer are quite moderate, normally 60F to 75F, and fog is common many days. This reduces the sun's intensity and also supplies a great amount of moisture. Humidity is also much higher than in inland climates. All these conditions combined reduce the moisture needs of plants. In fact, the additional humidity creates an environment that fosters many plant diseases. The absence of summer sun prevents heat-loving flowering plants such as crape myrtle from thriving. Frosts are rare, as is the case on the southern coast.

The Coast Ranges, groupings of ridges and hills, extend from Santa Maria to Eureka. These ridges and the river valleys within them greatly modify the climate of this region. The ranges and valleys nearest the coast tend to be cool and rainy in winter, with high humidity and frequent fog in summer. As you move inland, the daytime temperature increases and fog diminishes. Areas closest to the coast receive afternoon winds during summer. This is the climate of Oakland, Richmond, Hayward and Santa Cruz.

Thermal belts within the coastal ranges moderate winter temperatures in some places, so that cold-tender plants can often be grown. Locations within these thermal belts include Saratoga, Piedmont and the Berkeley Hills.

Cold-air basins are located in the many valleys along the coast and between mountain ranges. Cool air drains from the thermal belts above, lowering winter temperatures and causing late spring frosts. These areas include the cities of Hollister, Santa Rosa and

*Eschscholzia californica*, California poppy, is a popular wildflower throughout northern California.

**Average Annual Rainfall in Northern California and the Central Valley**

| | |
|---|---|
| Bakersfield | 6.10 |
| Berkeley | 23.10 |
| Bishop | 7.50 |
| Fresno | 9.40 |
| Livermore | 14.00 |
| Marysville | 20.70 |
| Merced | 11.80 |
| Napa | 22.70 |
| Palo Alto | 15.20 |
| Red Bluff | 23.10 |
| Sacramento | 15.90 |
| Salinas | 13.40 |
| San Jose | 13.95 |
| Santa Rosa | 29.10 |
| Visalia | 9.60 |
| Stockton | 14.10 |

Source: *Climate and Man*

Napa. Low temperatures generally drop into the the mid-20sF and occasionally to the mid-teens.

Rainfall away from the coast can be erratic enough to help cause drought conditions in certain years. Annual averages for selected cities include: Salinas, 13.40; Santa Maria, 14.10; San Jose, 13.95; Palo Alto, 15.20 inches. In addition, a sampling of last frost dates demonstrates how the coast modifies low temperatures: Oakland, January 11; San Jose, February 10; Salinas, March 17.

Much as on the Southern California coast, planting can be done year-round in most of this region. As you move away from the coast and low temperatures drop, do most planting in the fall. Wait until last spring frost has passed before setting out cold-tender plants.

**California's Great Central Valley—** This climate zone includes the Sacramento Valley in the north and the San Joaquin Valley in the south. It covers the heart of northern and central California, from Redding south through the cities of Sacramento, Fresno and Bakersfield. The valley stretches approximately 450 miles and is up to 50 miles wide. It is is completely encircled by mountain ranges.

Climates in the Central Valley are dominated by long, hot summers, with the highest temperatures at both the northern and southern ends of the valley. Daily highs reach well into the 100F range. As a rule, temperatures increase as you travel from north to south in the San Joaquin Valley and from south to north in the Sacramento Valley. As the elevation increases on the gradual slopes of the western side of the Sierra Nevada, winter lows become lower. Temperature extremes are more severe on the rugged inclines of the eastern slopes.

In low-lying valley areas, cold air drains down from slopes and creates "cold air lakes," lowering winter temperatures. These areas are also subject to dense *tule* fog in winter. This fog can actually serve as an insulating blanket for plants, moderating temperatures to reduce frosts. This is the climate of Bakersfield, Fresno and Merced.

The slopes from which the cold air drains create a climate zone composed of warm thermal belts located along the sides of the valley. This is the climate of Redding, Red Bluff and Porterville. At elevations of 500 to 700 feet, killing frosts are infrequent.

Another climate zone stretches from the San Francisco Bay Area east to Modesto and north to Sacramento, including Stockton, Lodi and Davis. Temperatures in this region are moderated by the marine air, fog and resulting higher humidity that flow inland from the San Francisco Bay. The Sacramento River Delta also has a moderating effect on temperatures, causing summers to be somewhat cooler and winters slightly warmer.

Average rainfall and average last spring frosts for selected cities in the valley are as follows: Maricopa, 5.70 inches, February 10; Bakersfield, 6.10 inches, February 21; Fresno, 9.40 inches, February 9; Merced, 11.80 inches, March 9; Stockton, 14.10 inches, February 14; Sacramento, 15.90 inches, February 6; and Davis, 16.45 inches, March 17.

Sow seed of wildflowers in fall to take advantage of winter rains. Plant hardy perennials and other hardy landscape plants in fall to early winter. After last spring frost, set out cold-tender annuals and perennials.

## Arizona

Arizona climates range from the cold-winter, high-elevation climates such as around Flagstaff, to the low-elevation Sonoran Desert around Phoenix. Flagstaff, at an elevation of about 7,000 feet, has a growing season (days between last and first frosts) of about 118 days. Average annual rainfall is about 20 inches. Cold temperatures decide which plants can be grown. Prescott, at 5,280 feet, has a definite winter season, but summers are hot. Low temperatures do not drop as low as in Flagstaff, so a greater selection of plants can be grown there.

**Arizona Low Desert—**This is the climate of Phoenix, Yuma and Casa Grande. It is typified by long, hot summers, mild winters and low rainfall. Phoenix is located in the Sonoran Desert at a 1,200-foot elevation. It is a subtropical desert, similar to Palm Springs in Southern California. Differences include more rainfall (7.60 inches each year compared to 3.70 in Palm Springs) and cooler summers. Daytime temperatures *average* 105F in summer in

Phoenix compared to Palm Springs' 110F to 115F. Winds are generally light, with the exception of high-velocity storms that can be part of the package of the summer rainy season.

Sow seed of wildflowers in fall to take advantage of winter rains. Plant hardy perennials and other hardy landscape plants from fall to early winter. After the last spring frost, set out cold-tender annuals and perennials. Killing frosts are few and the growing season is long. In Phoenix, the average last spring frost is February 5; at Yuma, on the Colorado River, it's January 12.

**Arizona Medium and High Deserts—** In the middle-elevation Sonoran Desert (2,200 feet) at Tucson, rainfall averages about 11.15 inches a year. Almost half falls during the summer months. Elevation has a great effect on rainfall. Every 1,000 feet in elevation increases rainfall annually by 4 to 5 inches. During a rainy summer, the foothills come alive as native plants respond to the moisture with fresh new growth and flowers.

Summer temperatures are generally 5F below those of Phoenix due to Tucson's higher elevation. Warmest temperatures occur in late June and early July, just prior to the onset of summer rains. Winter low temperatures restrict the use of many cold-tender, subtropical plants to sheltered microclimates and warm thermal belts on hillsides.

The planting seasons are the same as in the Arizona Low Desert. The growing season in Tucson is 252 days, with a last spring frost of March 15. Wickenburg, at 2,095 feet elevation, has a growing season of 242 days with last spring frost of March 21.

The high-elevation deserts of Arizona, 3,300 to 5,000 feet, include the cities of Kingman, Globe, Nogales, Sedona and Douglas. The increase in elevation brings a definite winter season with lower low temperatures and more days below 28F. Summers are hot but are not as extreme as in the low and middle deserts. Rainfall is greater in this region, averaging 15 inches and more per year. Cities in the southeastern part of the state tend to benefit most from the summer rainy season. For example, Nogales receives on the average almost 8 inches of rain dur-

ing July and August out of total annual rainfall of 16.10 inches; Douglas receives 6.15 inches during the same period out of its average of 12.80 inches a year.

Sow wildflower seed in fall. Plant cold-hardy plants in fall so they'll become established during the cool part of the year. Wait until after last spring frost before planting tender perennials and annuals. Last spring frost dates are averages, and late frosts are common. The last spring frost dates for cities in this zone are: Winslow, May 2; Globe, March 29; Nogales, March 30; and Douglas, April 8.

## New Mexico

New Mexico is a state with many climates, influenced by a rich mixture of high mesas (plateaus), mountains, canyons, valleys and mostly dry arroyos (washes). Elevations run from 3,000 feet along the southeastern border to about 14,000 feet atop the highest mountain peaks.

**New Mexico Medium and High Deserts—** In the southwestern and eastern sections of the state, as well as the Rio Grande Valley, the climate is typically medium to high desert, with elevations ranging from 3,300 to 4,500 feet and more. This is the climate of Albuquerque, Las Cruces, Hobbs and Roswell. Conditions here are similar to those in the high deserts of Arizona and California. Rainfall ranges from an average of 8.40 inches in Albuquerque to 14.40 inches in Hobbs. Summer rains account for almost half.

The higher elevations in New Mexico feature a cold-winter climate similar to that found throughout Colorado, Nevada and Utah. (See following.) Winter temperatures are lower than in Arizona and California; Albuquerque has more than 100 nights of sub-freezing weather.

Sow wildflower seed in fall. Plant cold-hardy plants in fall so they'll become established during the cool part of the year. Wait until after last spring frost before planting tender perennials and annuals. Last spring frost dates are averages, and late frosts are common. Be prepared to protect newly planted plants in spring. Last spring frosts for selected cities are: Albuquerque, April 13; Carlsbad, March 29; Santa Fe, April 24; and Roswell, April 7.

### Average Annual Rainfall in Arizona

| | |
|---|---|
| Casa Grande | 8.25 |
| Douglas | 12.80 |
| Flagstaff | 20.90 |
| Gila Bend | 5.80 |
| Globe | 16.50 |
| Grand Canyon | 16.50 |
| Kingman | 10.95 |
| Nogales | 16.10 |
| Phoenix | 7.60 |
| Prescott | 20.70 |
| Tucson | 11.15 |
| Willcox | 12.25 |
| Winslow | 8.35 |
| Yuma | 3.60 |

### Average Annual Rainfall in New Mexico

| | |
|---|---|
| Alamogordo | 11.25 |
| Albuquerque | 8.40 |
| Carlsbad | 13.15 |
| Clovis | 18.45 |
| Deming | 9.20 |
| Farmington | 8.45 |
| Roswell | 13.05 |
| Silver City | 16.85 |
| Santa Fe | 14.20 |
| Soccorro | 10.35 |

Source: *Climate and Man*

### Average Annual Rainfall in Nevada

| | |
|---|---|
| Carson City | 9.30 |
| Elko | 9.45 |
| Las Vegas | 4.85 |
| Reno | 7.75 |
| Tonopah | 4.70 |
| Winnemucca | 8.20 |

### Average Annual Rainfall in Utah

| | |
|---|---|
| Cedar City | 13.00 |
| Provo | 15.35 |
| Richfield | 8.40 |
| St. George | 8.75 |
| Salt Lake | 15.80 |

### Average Annual Rainfall in Colorado

| | |
|---|---|
| Boulder | 18.20 |
| Colorado Springs | 14.20 |
| Denver | 14.00 |
| Durango | 19.55 |
| Grand Junction | 8.75 |
| Pueblo | 11.55 |

Source: *Climate and Man*

*Ratibida columnifera*, Mexican hat, combines with boulders in this New Mexico garden. Red Mexican hat can be seen at lower left. In the background is *Linum perenne*, blue flax.

## Nevada, Utah and Colorado

The climate of these three states is largely governed by cold winters, with some exceptions. Snow is common at higher elevations and winter lows drop well below zero. Even in regions above 5,000 feet elevation, summers can get hot—temperatures over 100F are not uncommon.

The Great Basin Desert covers a great portion of Nevada and Utah.

Conditions here are almost as cold as in the surrounding high-elevation mountainous regions. Conditions in valleys and deserts are typically dry with bright sunshine and large swings in seasonal and day-to-night temperatures.

Lakes and rivers help modify cold temperatures. For example, the Great Salt Lake warms temperatures around Salt Lake City. The average last spring frost is April 13, and the growing

season is 192 days. Rainfall is 15.80 inches on the average each year. In the Virgin River Valley around St. George, Utah, the lower elevation (2,500 to 3,500 feet) increases the growing season to almost 200 days. The climate is similar to that of the Arizona high desert, although seasonal temperature extremes are greater. River valleys in western Colorado also moderate temperatures, such as around Grand Junction.

Set out plants in spring after danger of frost has passed. The growing season—days between last and first frosts—is usually under 150 days and can even be under 100 days (generally above 6,000 feet elevation). The last spring frost date fluctuates considerably, and gardeners must be aware that damaging late spring frosts are common. Premature fall frosts also damage plants that have not had time to gradually acclimate to the cooler temperatures. Creative use of microclimates can often make the difference between failure and success. Seek out sheltered, sunny, south and west exposures when locating more cold-tender plants. See pages 22 and 23 for more on microclimates.

**Southern Nevada**—Las Vegas and nearby Henderson are located in the eastern section of the Mojave Desert in southern Nevada. This area possesses a climate much different from that of the rest of Nevada, with conditions similar to the medium- elevation deserts of California. (See page 11.) At 2,000 feet, the elevation of Las Vegas is about the same as that of Tucson, Arizona, but the growing conditions are more harsh, with normal winter lows to mid-20sF. Soils here are often difficult-to-work caliche and have poor drainage. Summers are hot, with temperatures over 100F normally lasting from late May through August.

Annual rainfall is low, averaging less than 5 inches each year. Hot, drying winds can sap plants of moisture quickly. Windbreaks are helpful for plants as well as people.

Sow seed of wildflowers in fall to take advantage of meager winter rains. Plant hardy perennials and other hardy landscape plants in fall to early winter. After last spring frost, set out cold-tender annuals and perennials. The average last spring frost date for Las Vegas is March 16.

In Texas, the most popular wildflower (and the state flower) is the Texas bluebonnet, *Lupinus texensis*. A sea of bluebonnets surround this young girl.

## Average Annual Rainfall in Texas

| | |
|---|---|
| Abiline | 24.75 |
| Amarillo | 20.95 |
| Austin | 34.45 |
| Ft. Worth | 31.60 |
| El Paso | 8.55 |
| Laredo | 20.45 |
| Lubbock | 18.80 |
| Midland | 16.75 |
| San Angelo | 21.60 |
| San Antonio | 26.80 |
| Witchita Falls | 28.55 |

Source: *Climate and Man*

## Texas

Texas is the largest state within the continental United States, covering almost 266,000 square miles. It is an area of diverse climates and growing conditions. A broad look at the state divides it into four major geophysical regions: *Coastal Plains, North Central Plains*, the *Great Plains* and the *Trans-Pecos Mountain Area.*

This book concentrates on the more arid western half of Texas, approximately bounded by the 98th meridian, the so-called "rainline." This meridian is just east of Wichita Falls and San Antonio. Rainfall increases as you travel east across the state toward Louisiana and can be as plentiful as 50 inches per year in east Texas. Rainfall decreases as you travel west toward New Mexico and the Chihuahuan Desert. A look at rainfall averages of cities traveling east to west tells the story: San Antonio, 26.80 inches; San Angelo, 21.60 inches; Lubbock, 18.80 inches; Midland, 16.75 inches; El Paso, 8.55 inches. These figures are averages; rainfall in Texas can be erratic, with droughts lasting for months in some years.

The Great Plains region of Texas extends from the north and northwest as far south as Austin. Within the Great Plains are the High Plains of the Panhandle and the Edwards Plateau of southwest Texas.

**Texas High Plains—The Panhandle—** This is the northernmost portion of the state and the coldest, with elevations ranging from 3,000 to 4,700 feet. Amarillo and Lubbock are located here. Average rainfall is 17 to 20 inches per year, a large portion occurring in early summer. Average winter lows are 20F to 26F but lows well below zero have been recorded. The higher elevation moderates summer temperatures somewhat, with averages in the mid-90sF. Average last spring frost dates are: Amarillo, April 11, and Lubbock, April 12.

Wildflowers that do well here include *Penstemon* species, and *Aster tanacetifolius*, tahoka daisy.

**The Edwards Plateau—**This is the Hill Country, located in the heart of Texas. The southernmost portion reaches to the *Balcones Escarpment*, a geological fault line that follows a giant semicircle from Del Rio on the Rio Grande River to the Red River just west of Gainesville. The plateau extends as far west as the Pecos River. West of the river begins the Trans-Pecos area, described on page 19.

Large cities within this region tend to fall on geological and climatic boundaries (often limestone escarpments), making it precarious to define growing conditions. For example, San Angelo could be included here as well as in the Red Rolling Plains region. (See following.) Eastern portions of Austin and southern portions of San Antonio fall into the Blackland Prairie region.

Rainfall is substantial for cities closest to the 98th meridian, such as San Antonio, which receives an annual average of 26.80 inches. Del Rio, by comparison, located far to the southwest, receives 18.50 inches. Average last frost dates in spring are: San Antonio, February 24; and Del Rio, February 22.

A wide range of flowering plants are adapted to the Hill Country. In addition to those recommended for the High Plains, *Amsonia* species, blue Texas star, *Aster* species, aster, *Salvia* species, sage, and *Echinacea purpurea*, purple coneflower, are commonly grown.

**Red Rolling Plains—**Southeast of the high plains of the Panhandle lie the Red Rolling Plains. Together they mark the southern end of the Great Plains of the central U.S. The region gets its name from the reddish to pinkish color of the soils prevalent here.

As is typical in Texas, rainfall is higher in the eastern portion of the Rolling Red Plains: Wichita Falls, 28.55 inches; Abilene, 24.75 inches; San Angelo, 21.60 inches. May and September are normally rainy months. Summers are hot here; average temperatures reach up to 98F for San Angelo and Wichita Falls. This heat is often accompanied by drying winds, greatly increasing evaporation from plants and soil, necessitating additional irrigation. Average last spring frosts are: San Angelo, March 25; and Wichita Falls, March 22.

Flowering plants for this region include *Castilleja purpurea*, purple paintbrush, *Verbena bipinnatifida*, prairie verbena, and *Zinnia grandiflora*, yellow zinnia.

This Texas garden features *Castilleja* species (foreground), blue *Lupinus texensis*, Texas bluebonnet, and pinkish white *Oenothera* species, primrose.

**The Trans-Pecos Region**—This region is essentially a plateau with elevations ranging from 3,000 to 5,000 feet but reaching over 8,000 feet in mountain areas. The Chihuahuan Desert is located at lower elevations here. This is the climate of El Paso. Rainfall for the Trans-Pecos region is lowest in the state, averaging 6 to 12 inches a year. El Paso receives 8.55 inches on average. Rainfall is most prevalent in late summer. Summer temperatures are warm; in El Paso they average 95F. In mountain areas at higher elevations, summer temperatures are cooler.

Winter temperatures in El Paso tend to be mild by Texas standards, averaging 32F, but have dropped as low as 5F. The average last spring frost is March 21.

Wildflowers that do well in the higher-elevation regions surrounding El Paso do not necessarily do well in the city due to high temperatures in summer. *Berlandiera lyrata*, chocolate flower, *Psilostrophe* species, paperflower, and *Ratibida columnaris*, Mexican hat, are a few that accept the heat and adverse growing conditions.

# NEW WAYS
# WITH WILDFLOWERS

Wildflowers are traditionally associated with meadows—broad, sweeping vistas of flowers and grasses, blanketing acre after acre. Many gardeners relish the challenge of recreating a meadow in a home landscape setting, but wildflowers can be grown and enjoyed in so many other ways. They excel in natural borders, in rock gardens and interplanted between garden perennials and shrubs. Their colorful flowers and forms accept close-up viewing near outdoor living areas and entryways. They are also at home in the perimeter of the landscape as colorful, temporary ground covers for bare spots and along property lines.

When you select wildflowers with staggered blooming periods, you can enjoy wave after wave of dazzling, colorful displays. After the last of the annual wildflowers fade, perennial wildflowers begin to take center stage, continuing the color show up into fall.

The following pages describe new and old ways that wildflowers can be grown in home landscapes. Emphasis has been placed on natural garden designs. Included are ideas for large projects such as how to plant a mixed border with wildflowers, to creating intimate wildflower gardens in small-space areas around your home.

If you're new to wildflower gardening it's wise to start small and expand the scope of your garden after you learn which plants do best around your home. If children are in your family or neighborhood, invite them to participate in the process. They will be fascinated by the fast growth of the seedlings and most of all, the payoff of beautiful flowers. At the same time they'll learn a little about the ebb and flow of the seasons and how wildflowers fit into the grand scheme of things.

A simple border of wildflowers planted in masses brightens a garden path. Shown are white *Oenothera* species, primrose, gold *Eschscholzia californica*, California poppy, and blue *Phacelia campanularia*, California bluebell.

Above: Nothing quite matches the vibrant colors of wildflowers in full bloom. This mixture features gold *Eschscholzia californica*, California poppy, and blue *Lupinus* species.

## Selecting Sites

Picking the right locations for plants is important for any kind of garden. When planting wildflowers, it can be critical. For long-term plantings that are designed to evolve, such as a meadow or mixed border, the site must provide plants with what they need to grow or they will not thrive and reseed.

Get to know the conditions of the planting sites around your home, and select wildflowers to match them. Plants located in the right exposure and planted properly according to soil and water requirements are easier to grow, and your chances for success in the form of a beautiful display of wildflowers become much greater.

## Microclimates

Your home offers many potential locations for wildflower gardens. As you look around your front yard, side yard and back yard areas, you'll notice differences in the amount of sunshine, temperatures and frequency and intensity of the wind. These small climate variations are called *microclimates*. Every home lot is different, and microclimates change continually as the plants on site grow, increasing shade and wind protection.

Microclimates are more complex in hilly terrain. Cool air flows down hillsides during the evening hours, lowering temperatures in its path. If the flow of cool air is blocked by a hedge, wall or other barrier, the air pools and temperatures drop even

An understanding of microclimates will help you learn how to select plants that are adapted to the various growing conditions around your home. These *Verbena* species are among the best plants for hot, sunny western exposures, such as the one shown here. Shade from trees supply relief from the intense afternoon sun.

lower. It is for this reason that you should avoid placing cold-tender plants in low-lying areas. Areas that stretch laterally across slopes, above valleys but below the crest, especially if they face toward the sunny south, are *thermal belts*. Temperatures in a thermal belt remain much warmer, as much as 10F, than in the valley bottom below. If your home lot is in a thermal belt, you can plant earlier in the spring season. It also allows you to grow more cold-tender plants than generally recommended for your climate.

One of the easiest ways to learn about microclimates is to observe them around your home and around your neighborhood. Exposures receiving southeast or eastern morning sun are *warm*. By comparison, southwest or south afternoon sun locations are *hot*. If the sun reflects off walls or paving, temperatures climb even higher and soils dry out more rapidly. Plants located here must be tolerant of heat and intense sunlight. On the north side, you'll notice that temperatures are cooler and the soil is often more moist. This exposure does not receive as much sunshine, especially in winter. Most wildflowers will not thrive here, except for those that are adapted to deep shade.

The majority of wildflowers require six to eight hours of sun each day,

although some are adapted to shaded locations. Sunlight is highly variable depending on your climate and the time of day plants are exposed to the sun. Eight hours of sunlight is not nearly as intense in a cool, coastal garden as in the sunny desert. Garden plants in Phoenix, Arizona, for example, are almost always appreciative of afternoon shade. The Gallery of Wildflowers, pages 37 to 110, lists the preferred exposures for each plant.

Trees and shrubs around your home provide mixed blessings. They can produce desirable shade, turning a too-hot western exposure into a tolerable planting area. Then again, roots of many trees and shrubs invade your planting beds, stealing water and nutrients from your flowering plants. Be prepared to compensate with additional moisture.

After you've reviewed potential planting sites around your home, select locations that will support the cultural requirements of the wildflowers you want to grow. Of these, pick sites that offer you, your family and visitors the most impact. This is one of the fun parts of designing a garden. Spend some time visualizing how your plant combinations will look in a number of locations. If possible, pick a location that can be viewed from inside your home as well as outside.

Far left: Front yard is planted with natural drifts of pink *Penstemon parryi*, penstemon, blue *Lupinus* species, lupine, and yellow *Baileya multiradiata*, desert marigold. Flowers bloom through spring and into early summer.

Above: If your wildflowers are located at the perimeter of your landscape, rabbits, squirrels and other small animals may become as interested in the progress of your planting as you. Sturdy fencing will help protect your plants, but is seldom a cure.

Above: *Encelia farinosa*, brittle bush, are located in this landscape's low-water zone. They add color for a long period during spring, while also protecting this steep slope from erosion.

Opposite: Wildflowers in simple combinations can be very dramatic, such as these gold *Eschscholzia californica*, California poppy, and blue *Phacelia campanularia*, California bluebell.

Opposite: A *mixture* of wildflowers has its own appeal, when splashes of multiple bright colors are combined in one planting.

## Wildflowers and Water Use

An important aspect of site selection is the availability of water as well as the water requirements of the plants you want to grow. Most wildflowers require moist (not soaking wet) soil to germinate and regular amounts of water for several weeks following to become established. Unless you live in a high-rainfall region, you will need to irrigate planting sites at least until seedlings have developed into young plants. If water is unavailable, you are at the mercy of seasonal rains. The appearance of your garden could be spectacular or abysmal, depending on the whims of the rain gods.

Grouping your wildflowers according to their moisture requirements, called *hydrozoning*, is a simple landscaping principle but is highly useful to gardeners in the arid West. Zoning plants allows you to budget water use, limiting the number of high-water-use plants to small areas close to outdoor living spaces. Grouping plants also reduces weeding, trimming and grooming. Natural garden designs, discussed in the following, is an excellent way to put the hydrozoning concept into practice.

Three water-use zones are recommended for home landscapes:

**Low-Water Zone**—Placed farthest from your home. Select plants that, after becoming estab-lished, can live on rainfall (not always possible in extremely low-rainfall, hot-summer clmates) or with minimum summer irrigation. Or grow annuals that will die out during hot weather, allowing the area to remain unplanted (and eliminating irrigation altogether) during the hot summer months.

**Moderate-Water Zone**—Plants that require some irrigation but are not water-greedy. Most are vigorous growers that produce flowers equal to or surpassing those of high-water plants. Note that the vast majority of wildflowers fall into the moderate-water and low-water zones.

**High-Water Zone**—Plants requiring the most water. Plant in small quantities and group closely together to get the most out of water applied. Grouping also increases humidity, reducing evaporation. A high-water zone is often called a *mini-oasis*. Like an oasis in the desert, it is a spot near outdoor living areas where you can enjoy your favorite plants and their nuances of fragrance, color and texture. It serves as a focal point and gives your eyes and senses a coolness that contrasts nicely with the surrounding landscape.

# Design Basics

*Color, form* and *texture* are three basic elements of design you should consider when combining and positioning plants. Other design factors are *scale*—how the sizes of plants and the garden relate to the whole scene of home and landscape— and *balance*—keeping planting beds in proportion in mass and size with one another.

## Color

Wildflowers come in almost every color imaginable, with seasonal bloom periods to match. Because color is the most dramatic design feature at your disposal, it takes some planning to achieve the effect you want. For example, you may want a sensational display of color during late spring or summer, with a profusion of plants coming into bloom at once. Or you might want your garden to ebb and flow with color as certain species bloom and others fade, providing interest throughout the year. Mixed colors can be created with wildflower mixes. Plants can also be arranged in separate blocks and bands of color. The chart on pages 38 and 39 will assist you with your planning, supplying the plant sizes, flower colors and bloom periods of plants described in this book.

As you make your color selections, keep in mind that color varies according to the surroundings and exposure. Walls, buildings, garden structures, background plants and even the sky absorb or reflect color. For example, a white wall in the background will cause light-colored flowers to lose their impact.

The quality of light varies according to where you live. Pastel and light-colored flowers look best in the cool, even light of a coastal garden. In the sun-drenched desert, these colors lose their intensity. The bright, warm-colored sunlight creates a scene better suited to rich reds, purples, magentas and yellows.

Color helps define a mood. For a garden that evokes calmness, select and mass plants with complementary foliage colors and textures and similar flower colors. Combine a few plant species in natural-shaped drifts, rather than a smattering of many colors, to enhance the calming effect. Blue and

gray flower colors are good choices. Blending colors as well as forms and textures works especially well with small gardens where a simple design visually expands the garden space.

For a more dramatic effect, create eye-catching combinations with color opposites. A good example of this is yellow flowers planted with violet or blue. You can test color combinations by planting fast-blooming annual bedding plants in containers. Before you commit to a mass planting, move them around to see how they look together, then make adjustments to color, amount and placement.

## Form

The shape and form of plants, whether mounding, vertical or creeping, influence the appearance of a design. The relative mature height and spread of plants must also be kept in scale with one another. If positioned incorrectly, taller, more aggressive plants will block the view of smaller plants or even smother them.

Annual wildflowers are temporary plants; most provide color and substance in the landscape from spring to early summer. To maintain the

form of your wildflower border or meadow, include permanent evergreen landscape plants. Small shrubs, ornamental grasses and perennials can be combined with your wildflowers. Another simple way is to include boulders and rocks in your design for visual interest while wildflowers are absent. See photos, page 29.

Form in a design can create interest by gradually directing attention to an accent plant or grouping. This is a *focal point*, determined by massing one plant species at a particular position, perhaps at the apex of a curve. Plants of a contrasting color or stature can accomplish the same thing.

## Texture

Texture means many things in a landscape design. Close up, it defines the surface of leaves and flowers, such as fine-textured, lacy leaves or large, coarse leaves. It can also relate to the landscape as viewed from a distance when plant forms present a fine or coarse appearance.

As you would blend colors, blend plants with similar textures. Combine plants with similar fine-textured foliage. For contrast, place them near groups of coarse-foliaged plants.

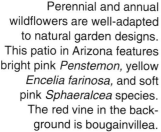

Perennial and annual wildflowers are well-adapted to natural garden designs. This patio in Arizona features bright pink *Penstemon*, yellow *Encelia farinosa*, and soft pink *Sphaeralcea* species. The red vine in the background is bougainvillea.

# Natural Garden Design

Native wildflowers are perfect choices for a natural garden setting. They evoke the atmosphere of the surrounding region, including its indigenous colors, textures and forms. Plants are combined to suggest a natural scene, drawing inspiration from the nearby countryside.

Natural design plantings with wildflowers are well suited, both culturally and aesthetically, to the water-saving principles discussed on page 24, using low-water and moderate-water-use plants. A small, high-water traditional garden can be retained, if desired, as a private oasis.

Many varied natural environments exist in the arid West, from the cool, soft-lighted coast to the sharp lines and bright contrasts of the deserts to the rugged, rocky foothills. Natural gardening involves understanding the unique character of plants and terrain that occur in the undeveloped areas around your home. By including native wildflowers and other native plants, the garden becomes a living bridge to your surroundings.

Here are some additional ideas to assist you in creating a natural landscape design.

**Observe Native Wildflowers in Natural Settings**—Wildflowers still exist in nature, but urban development has reduced native stands dramatically. Visit preserves such as the Antelope Valley California Poppy Reserve in Lancaster, California, where you can view wildflowers in a natural state. Arboretums and botanical gardens throughout the West offer many opportunities to learn about native wildflowers. Plants at arboretums and botanical gardens will be accurately identified. Many of these gardens also have undeveloped areas as well as interpretive displays and demonstration gardens that show examples of native landscapes. Take photos of plants and scenes that interest you to serve as inspiration for your own garden.

**Develop a Scrapbook of Natural Scenes**—Many people collect ideas when planning an interior remodel or when building a new home. The same principle works for outdoor projects. Clip photos of native gardens or natural scenes from magazines, or mark book pages to refer to later on. Regional home and garden publications and the local Sunday newspaper also supply ideas. Keep a garden journal and write down the names of favorite wildflowers and why you like them.

**Get to Know Your Region's "Sense of Place"**—This requires an understanding of the unique native vegetation, terrain, rock formations and even architectural history of your area. Every place has these distinct characteristics, whether you live in the desert, in the mountains or on the

In this New Mexico garden, a natural planting works well on a small scale. These *Penstemon* are attractive against a brightly painted window frame.

coast. A sense of place provides a focus, helping you include the plants and elements that fit with local traditions and history. Even within general climate zones, there are many differences. For example, the low-elevation, subtropical desert climate of Palm Springs is much different from the low-elevation desert climate in Phoenix.

**Select Plants with Casual Growth Habits**—In addition to wildflowers, include permanent landscape plants that do not require extensive pruning. For those native shrubs and trees on site, resist the urge to prune them heavily. Allow them to grow unpruned into their natural forms. Perennial ornamental grasses are other excellent choices. Their informal shapes, textures and colors fit in a natural scene. When assisted by the wind, they add sound and movement.

**Space Plants and Materials Randomly**—Place plants in groups or clusters as they would appear in nature. Allow plenty of depth and space for the planting area. Create natural, undulating earth berms and rolling terrain to add interest to a common flat lot. Space stones and boulders randomly to support the effect. See following.

## Rocks and Boulders in the Natural Landscape

Boulders and rocks provide a dramatic link to the natural dry washes and rock-studded hillsides common in the arid West. The form, color and texture of boulders provide an ideal setting for native and adapted low-water-use plants. In addition to their aesthetic value, boulders create moisture-retentive areas for plant roots. And, as garden seasons progress and plants move through flowering cycles and into dormancy or die, the boulders provide an unchanging stability to the scene.

Choices for rocks and boulders should be small (1-1/2 to 2 feet in diameter), medium (2 to 2-1/2 feet) and large (3 to 4 feet). Arrange them in odd numbers in random clusters. Bury at least one-fourth of each rock so it appears as it would in the natural environment. Bury some rocks more deeply than others, arranging them to suggest the natural rock formations common to your area. Avoid huge boulders for small-area gardens much

as you would avoid using towering trees or wide-spreading shrubs. Don't try to include too many kinds of rocks or other elements.

Boulders 1 to 2 feet in diameter can often be handled with a heavy-duty two-wheeled dolly. Due to their size and weight, larger boulders must be set in place with a crane or heavy equipment. Hire a landscaping firm to do this after all rough grading is completed. Stake the location of groupings, digging out holes in advance. After positioning, backfill around the bases of boulders.

Vertical accent plants with sword-shaped leaves are dramatic when combined with boulders. Low-growing wildflowers can flow over the ground and around the boulders. Consider grasslike plants with native shrubs, ground covers or perennials planted on the sides of slopes and among the boulders. Carpets of *Eschscholtzia californica*, California poppy, *Linum grandiflorum* 'Rubrum', scarlet flax, or *Oenothera* species, primrose, stabilize the soil and provide color and interesting textures.

**Dry Stream Beds**—A simulated dry stream bed helps give your natural landscape a focal point. In addition to being a design element, it can perform a valuable function by channeling excess rainwater runoff through the landscape or into retention basins. Add masses of wildflowers in clumps and drifts near the stream bed, simulating what might occur in nature.

Stream beds are usually 1 to 1-1/2 feet deep and 3 to 6 feet wide, depending on space available and length of run. Use boulders of various sizes in clusters on the edges of banks. Add small, 1- to 3-inch pebbles or cobblestones to stabilize soil between boulders in the bottom and sides of the stream-bed swale. Imagine the action of rainfall runoff on the soil, rocks and gravel and arrange them accordingly.

**Rock Gardens**—Rock gardens differ from boulder gardens in that they are usually developed on mounds, terraces and hillsides to stabilize the soil. They are best kept low profile, emulating natural rock outcroppings. Interplant with low-growing perennial and annual wildflowers as well as herbs.

Rocks should be combined carefully to create cool, moist, sheltered pockets for plant roots. Improve the soil among rocks by thoroughly mixing in organic amendments. A drip irrigation system can be installed to water perennial plants. The drip emitters provide small amounts of water on a regular basis to plant roots. This avoids overhead sprinkling and reduces weed growth and water stains. Conceal the drip tubing beneath the soil or cover with a mulch such as decomposed granite.

Above left: Masses of *Eschscholzia californica*, California poppy, add color to a dry stream bed.

Above: Rocks and boulders are arranged to complement wildflowers and perennials at home entry. After the majority of flowering has passed in late spring, the rocks provide continuing interest to the scene.

Opposite, top: Wildflowers planted in drifts create a striking "wildflower hill." *Linaria reticulata*, toadflax, is in the foreground. White flowers are *Dimorphotheca* species, cape marigold.

Opposite, below: A gentle slope is protected from erosion and made more attractive with wildflower planting. Red flowers are *Linum grandiflorum* 'Rubrum', red flax.

## Creating a Mixed Border

A border, as its name suggests, is a planting (usually an edge or strip) around a lawn area or against a wall or hedge. A *mixed border* is a similar design, but follows the natural garden philosophy discussed on pages 27 to 29. It can include annual and perennial wildflowers, ornamental grasses and small flowering shrubs.

The shape of a mixed border is highly dependent on the individual site, unlike geometrically shaped, formal perennial borders and planting beds. Most are kept to 4 to 6 feet deep to make it easier to plant, weed, water and maintain plants. If beds are much narrower, it is easy to overplant them and plants tend to crowd one another.

Keep the mature sizes in mind as you select plants for the border. Pick low-growing species 6 to 12 inches high for the edge of the area, species with heights of 1 to 3 feet for middle areas, and the tallest species, 3 to 5 feet, as accent groups and as a background against walls or fences.

Newly planted perennials often take two or even three seasons before plants fill out and produce many flowers. Including fast-growing annual wild-flowers in the planting scheme the first year provides color and interest while perennial plants are maturing. Select annual wildflowers with colors that will complement the flower colors of your perennials. Low-growing, compact varieties are preferred, but space them 12 to 18 inches away from perennial plants. Most annuals are aggressive growers and are quite capable of smothering the basal growth of slower-growing perennials. (This is particularly true during early spring when most perennials are dormant.) Thin annuals early in the spring to give the perennials room to grow. If annuals are allowed to grow unchecked, they can retard the recovery of perennial plants.

There are several ways to make laying out a planting design easier. Some gardeners use graph paper and sketch designs to scale to create their planting schemes. Marking the area with sand or gypsum will distinguish sections of separate plants or colors. Or use the handle of a hoe or rake to trace patterns in the soil. A design where sections flow into one another rather than stop-and-start angles is more pleasing and natural. Overlap separate colors to create a gentle blending. The illustrations on pages 34 and 35 show some examples.

Individual species of wildflowers planted in masses create a different effect compared to a wildflower mix, opposite page. Shown are white *Oenothera* species, primrose, gold *Eschscholzia californica*, California poppy, and blue *Phacelia campanularia*, California bluebell.

# A Wildflower Meadow

Recreating a meadow as part of your landscape is a popular method of growing wildflowers. A meadow of mixed wildflowers is especially appealing if the background is simple, such as green foothills or grove of trees. But keep in mind that meadows do require a fair amount of space, water and time to create. Those strikingly photogenic meadows that occur in nature have evolved after thousands of years and may require just the right amounts of moisture and cold to bloom to perfection each year.

Most meadow gardens are composed of a mixture of annual and perennial wildflowers and various kinds of grasses. In a natural meadow the grasses actually make up 50 to 80 percent of the meadow plants. The grasses help control soil erosion and provide support for the taller wild-flowers. They also effectively reduce the number of weeds that can establish and overrun the meadow.

Select your site carefully, following the information provided at the beginning of this chapter. Also refer to Wild-flowers: The Basics, pages 113 to 124. If your meadow will cover a large area, select a site that has not previously been infested with weeds. Control weeds following the instructions for minor weed invasions on page 116. Select wildflowers adapted to your location; those native to your specific area are best.

**Selecting Seed**—Wildflowers are available in prepackaged, regionally adapted mixes. Some are definitely more regional than others. If you purchase one of these, get one that applies to your *vegetational* region: your elevation, specific terrain and climate zone. If you live in Tucson, a mix formulated for the middle-elevation Sonoran Desert is more likely to succeed than one formulated for the Southwest U.S.

The best method is to create your own mix of native perennial and annual wildflowers. Most adapted plants will reseed and reestablish the following year, rather than being a one-year flash in the pan. After selecting species, calculate the amount of seed required to cover the proposed area. Seeding rates for 100 square feet, 500 square feet and 1 acre are supplied for each wildflower in the Gallery of Wildflowers, pages 37 to 110.

Note: The more wildflower species you select to cover a given area, the more you need to reduce the amount of recommended seed. Because the weight of wildflower seeds varies considerably, this can be a tricky proposition. For example, one pound of seed of *Linaria maroccana*, toadflax, contains almost 7 million seeds. One pound of *Lupinus texensis*, Texas blue-bonnet, contains 16,000 seeds. As a guide, if you plant two species, reduce the recommended amount by one-half. If you plant four species, apply one-fourth the recommended amount, and so on.

This wildflower meadow was planted from a mixture formulated by a seed company, regionalized for the area. For best results, buy a mix that most closely matches your area, or create a custom mix of wildflowers native to your region.

Planting in small-space locations such as this one at the base of a planter is a fun way to experiment with wildflowers. These are blue *Phacelia campanularia*, California bluebell, red *Penstemon* (flower buds), and a light pink, cultivated variety of *Eschscholzia californica*, California poppy.

**Meadow Maintenance**—The first year, annual species will steal the show with their fast-blooming flowers. Perennial species require two or three years to bloom. Your maintenance goal is to encourage the annual wildflowers to reseed after the first year and beyond and bring the perennial species to flowering the following year or year after. It is possible to plant perennial species from containers purchased at the nursery to establish the meadow faster. Be sure to space plants randomly. At the end of the season when flowers cease to bloom, follow the maintenance practices as recommended on pages 123 to 124.

# Small-Space Gardens

Wildflowers are particularly well adapted to small, irregular spaces around your home. A small garden, 50 to 100 square feet, is recommended for first-time wildflower gardeners. It is easier to manage and you learn which wildflowers perform best. As you gain experience you can take on larger projects.

It is easy to create free-form planting patterns with simple combinations of two, three or more kinds of plants. Here are some ideas for small-space gardens:

- In masses alongside walk or path to the front door
- In entry court at front door
- As ribbon border along walkway or driveway
- For quick fill-in color around newly planted shrubs
- In narrow spaces such as side yards between house and fence
- As a mass backdrop around a pool or spa
- Along a drainage swale or simulated dry creekbed
- On a slope for erosion control
- In front yard as replacement for lawn or to reduce lawn area
- Under low windows
- In raised beds for a cutting garden
- In containers or window boxes on patio, on deck or at entry

## Growing Wildflowers in Containers

Most wildflowers can be grown in containers. It's mostly a matter of keeping the plant's height and spread in scale with the size of the container, and planting in soil that provides good drainage.

One of the greatest benefits of container gardening is mobility. You can move plants to suit the time and place. Plants in flower can be displayed in a highly visible location, such as near the patio or entry. After blooms are spent, plants can be moved off center stage until they bloom again.

A disadvantage of plants in containers is the additional water they require. Compared to in-ground plantings, the soil dries out much more quickly. Moisture loss can be extremely rapid

in hot, windy locations. In hot-summer regions, plants in containers might need watering every day. In these instances, drip irrigation is a wise way to water.

A container at least 16 to 18 inches wide and 12 to 18 inches deep is usually adequate for both shallow and deep-rooted species. Note that winter cold will penetrate container soil more than in-ground plantings. Consider using wood half-barrels, available at home centers and nurseries. Check the thickness of wood and be sure joints are tight before you make your purchase. These barrels are heavy after they're filled with soil and can be difficult to move without a dolly, so position them accordingly.

Provide container plants with afternoon shade during the summer months to help reduce water need. This is often a necessity in hot-summer regions. If possible, locate plants where they receive exposure to the less-intense morning sun, receiving shade during the hot afternoon hours. Turning the container one-quarter turn each week helps keep plant growth even.

**Soil for Containers**—Soil mixes for wildflowers should be loose and well draining. Several kinds are available. Some gardeners use a sterile potting soil straight out of the bag. Others mix the potting soil with equal parts of sand and ground bark or peat moss. The added weight of the sand is helpful in windy regions, preventing plants from being blown over. A house plant potting soil is lightweight and recommended for hanging plants and baskets.

# A Home Landscape with Wildflowers

This landscape plan provides some ideas on how to include wildflowers around your home. In this plan, the Front Garden features a majority of wildflowers that will bloom profusely the first season after planting. Such a design is perfect for a new home that does not yet have a landscape. This plan also is effective in providing temporary color and coverage for a newly renovated landscape until more permanent plants can attain size and substance.

The Rear Garden features combinations of perennials and annuals for longer-term displays. These are more permananent plants. With a few years growth they will develop into an attractive natural border beyond the lawn area. Plants in this design have been selected and arranged to provide interesting, colorful views from the covered porch area outdoors, as well as from inside through the large, glass patio doors.

Plants in the Rear Garden were chosen with mature sizes in mind to provide a layered, blended appearance. In the foreground, for example, is *Coreopsis auriculata* 'Nana', which grows to just 6 inches high. Also in the foreground is *Gaillardia aristata*, blanketflower, with a mature height of 1-1/2 feet. *Salpiglossis sinuata*, painted tongue (3 feet high), and *Rudbeckia hirta*, black-eyed Susan (4 feet high), are placed behind these smaller species. All plants can grow to mature flowering stage without blocking the view of one another.

## Making Your Own Design

The plants in this plan are well adapted throughout the West. Use them as a guide to create a design for your own home landscape. For best results, become familiar with the growing conditions of each planting site around your home, then select wildflowers to match them. The cultural preferences of each plant are provided in the Gallery of Wildflowers, pages 37 to 110. Also refer to the Plant Selection Guide on pages 38 and 39 as a quick reference to plant colors, mature sizes and seasonal bloom periods.

Once you have have decided on locations and made a list of plants suited to them, you can create your own designs. Begin by drawing your home and landscape site on graph paper, using the squares to equal a unit of measurement. Include your house, property lines, walks, driveways and existing trees and shrubs. This drawing becomes your base plan.

Now cover it with tracing paper and sketch in the locations, sizes and shapes of potential wildflower beds. Now is the time to experiment. Use color pencils to envision combinations of flower colors. Consider how the gardens might appear from indoors as well as outdoors. After your ideas begin to make sense, make a final design similar to the one shown here. Accurately measure each garden site to figure out the number of plants and amount of seed required to fill the allotted space. Seeding rates for 100 square feet, 500 square feet and per acre are provided for each genera in the Gallery of Wildflowers.

Keep detailed records of planting dates, amount of seed planted, when seeds germinated and flowers first appeared. Record successes as well as failures. This information will be a valuable reference for next year's garden.

### Rear Garden

Total plants and seed required

**A.** *Chrysanthemum frutescens,* marguerite—2 plants (gallon size)

Option: *Euryops* species, golden euryops—2 plants (gallon size)

**B.** *Salpiglossis sinuata,* painted tongue—5 grams of seed (about 25 plants in each area)

**C.** *Gaillardia aristata,* blanketflower—25 plants (quart or gallon size)

**D.** *Asclepias tuberosa,* butterfly weed—9 plants (gallon or 5-gallon size)

**E.** *Kochia scoparia,* summer cypress—5 plants (one seed packet)

**F.** *Rudbeckia hirta,* black-eyed Susan—12 plants (quart or gallon size)

**G.** *Coreopsis auriculata* 'Nana', coreopsis—28 plants (quart or gallon size)

**H.** *Eustoma grandiflorum,* Texas bluebell—18 plants (quart or gallon size)

## Front Garden

Total plants and seed required

**F.** *Rudbeckia hirta,* black-eyed Susan—8 plants (gallon size)

**J.** *Oenothera* species, evening primrose—62 plants (quart or gallon size)

**K.** *Eschscholzia californica,* California poppy—2 ounces of seed with *Phacalecia campanularia,* California bluebell—1 ounce of seed

**L.** *Linum grandiflorum* 'Rubrum', scarlet flax—4 ounces of seed with *Liatris spicata* 'Kobold', gayfeather—1 ounce of seed

**M.** *Aquilegia* species, columbine—24 plants (gallon size)

**N.** *Mimulus cardinalis,* monkey flower—24 plants (gallon size). Plant in foreground with *Aquilegia*

**O.** *Encelia farinosa,* brittle bush—9 plants (gallon size)

## East Garden

**I.** *Dimorphotheca sinuata,* African daisy—10 ounces of seed

Or plant wildflower seed mixture, formulated for your region

## West Garden

**I.** *Dimorphotheca sinuata,* African daisy—12 ounces seed

Or plant wildflower seed mixture, formulated for specific region

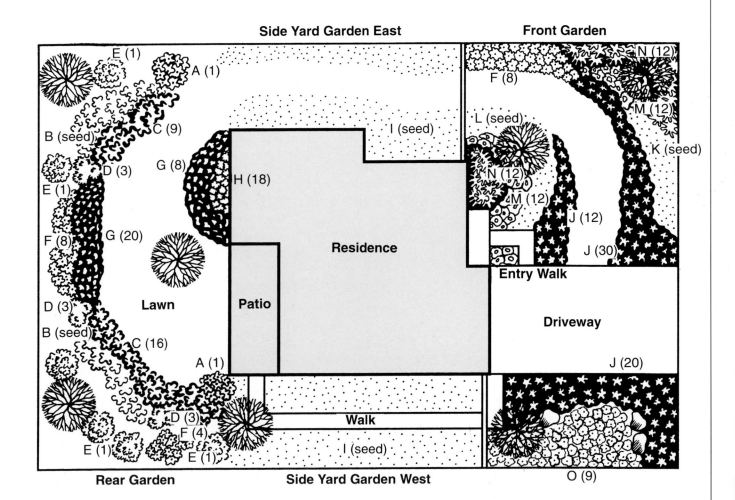

# GALLERY
# OF WILDFLOWERS

The unique and varied climates of the West provide challenges and opportunities for growing wildflowers. On the following pages, more than 180 annual and perennial wildflower species are shown and described in detail, including their flower colors, foliage, height and width, blooming season and landscape uses. Each description also includes a map that shows where in the West the plant is adapted to grow. Consider these maps a general guide. In many instances wildflowers can be grown successfully throughout the West. Note that plants are listed in alphabetical order by botanical name. If you know a plant only by its common name, refer to the index on pages 126 to 128.

Before selecting wildflowers, do a thorough evaluation of the growing conditions around your home. The wildflowers you want to grow should be adapted to the sun, soil and moisture you will supply them. The fact column located beside each description lists the plant's vital statistics and its cultural requirements.

Consider, too, what you want to accomplish with your wildflowers. Do you want color through many seasons, or a single spectacular display orchestrated to bloom during late spring? The Plant Selection Guide on pages 38 and 39 provides the mature heights, bloom periods and flower colors for each wildflower genus included in this book.

Wildflowers, for the most part, are low- to moderate-water-use plants, but they do require regular, consistent moisture to germinate and become established. The suggested water-use rating given each wildflower in the fact column, whether it is high, moderate or low, should be used as a guide *after* plants are established and growing. For most annual wildflowers little water will be required after flowering reaches it peak.

*Papaver nudicaule,* Iceland poppy, make a dramatic scene when backlit by the sun.

Above: A single California poppy plant demonstrates a strong will to grow, needing only a small fissure in this rock to reach flowering stage.

# Plant Selection Guide

| BOTANICAL NAME | HEIGHT (IN FEET) | FLOWER COLORS | SEASONS OF BLOOM (Winter – Spring – Summer – Fall) |
|---|---|---|---|
| Abronia villosa | <1 | Pur | Winter–Spring |
| Achillea | <1-3 | P, W, Y | Spring–Summer |
| Aquilegia | 1-1/2-3 | B&W, B-L, R&Y, Y | Spring–Summer |
| Argemone platyceras | 3 | W&Y | Spring–Summer |
| Asclepias | 2-3 | O, W | Spring–Summer |
| Aster | 2-4 | L-B, Pur, R | Summer–Fall |
| Baileya multiradiata | 1-1-1/2 | Y | Spring–Fall |
| Berlandiera lyrata | 1-1-1/2 | Y | Spring–Summer |
| Brachycome iberidifolia | 1 | B, P, W | Spring–Summer |
| Bupleurum rotundifolium | 2 | G, Y | Summer |
| Campanula | <1-6 | B, L, P, W | Spring–Summer |
| Castilleja | 1-1-1/2 | O-R, P, Pur, R, Y | Spring–Summer |
| Centaurea cyanus | 1-3 | B, P, R, W | Spring–Summer |
| Cerastium tomentosum | <1 | W | Spring–Summer |
| Chrysanthemum | 1-1/2-3 | O, P, W, Y, Y&W | Spring–Fall |
| Cirsium | 4-6 | P-W | Spring–Fall |
| Clarkia | <1-3 | L, P, O, Pur, W | Spring–Summer |
| Collinsia heterophylla | 2 | L&W | Spring–Summer |
| Consolida ambigua | 3-4 | B, P, R, W | Spring–Summer |
| Coreopsis | <1-3 | R&Y, Y | Spring–Summer |
| Cosmos | 2-7+ | O, P, R, W | Summer–Fall |
| Datura | 2-1/2+ | L, W | Summer–Fall |
| Delphinium | 3-6 | R | Spring |
| Dianthus | <1-2 | P, Pur, R | Spring–Fall (intermittent) |
| Digitalis purpurea | 2-4+ | Pur | Summer |
| Dimorphotheca sinuata | 1 | O, Y, W | Winter–Spring |
| Dyssodia tenuiloba | 1 | Y | Summer–Fall |
| Echinacea | 3-5 | Pur, Pur-P | Summer–Fall |
| Encelia | 3-4 | Y | Winter–Spring |
| Eschscholzia | 1-1-1/2 | O, Y, W | Spring–Summer |
| Euphorbia | 2-3 | GF, R&W, W | Summer–Fall |
| Eustoma grandiflorum | 1-1-1/2 | B, P, Pur, W | Summer |
| Gaillardia | 1-1/2-2 | R, R&Y, Y | Summer–Fall |
| Gazania splendens | <1-1 | O, R, Y | Spring–Summer |
| Gilia | 2 | B, B-Pur, R | Spring–Summer |
| Gypsophila | 3-3-1/2 | W | Summer |
| Helianthus | 8-10+ | Y, R | Summer |
| Hesperis matronalis | 2-3 | L, Pur, W | Summer |
| Hyptis emoryi | 3-10 | L | Winter–Spring |
| Ipomopsis | 2-5 | R, R&Y | Spring–Summer |
| Kallstroemia grandiflora | 1 | O&R | Spring–Summer |
| Kochia scoparia | 6 | Foliage (Green) | Summer–Fall |
| Lasthenia glabrata | <1-2 | Y | Spring–Summer |
| Lathyrus | 1-1/2-2 | R-pur, W | Summer |
| Lavatera trimestris | 3-6 | P, R-P, W | Summer |

Use this chart to help plan your garden, selecting wildflowers according to size, flower color and bloom seasons. Note that mature sizes, bloom periods and even flower color will vary according to your climate and the season. In general, plants tend to flower *later* into summer in coastal regions, and begin *earlier* in late winter and spring in mild, hot-climate areas.

| BOTANICAL NAME | HEIGHT (IN FEET) | FLOWER COLORS | SEASONS OF BLOOM |
|---|---|---|---|
| Layia platyglossa | <1-1-1/2 | Y&W | Spring |
| Liatris | 1-1/2-5 | R-P, Pur, W | Summer–Fall |
| Linanthus grandiflorus | <1-1 | P, L, L-W, R, Y | Spring |
| Linaria | <1-2 | P, Pur, R, Y | Spring |
| Linum | 1-2 | B, R | Spring |
| Lobelia cardinalis | 1-6 | R | Spring–Summer |
| Lobularia maritima | 1 | Pur, W | Winter–Fall |
| Lupinus | 1-1/2-4 | B, B&W, P, Pur, Y | Spring |
| Lychnis chalcedonica | 3 | O, P, R, W | Spring–Summer |
| Malcolmia maritima | <1-1 | L, P, W, Y | Spring–Summer |
| Mentzelia lindleyi | 1-4 | R&Y, Y | Spring |
| Mimulus cardinalis | 2-4 | O-R | Summer |
| Mirabilis | 1-1/2-3 | P, Pur-R, R, Y, W | Summer–Fall |
| Moluccella laevis | 1-1/2-2 | G | Spring |
| Monarda | 1-1/2-3 | P, R, W | Spring–Summer |
| Myosotis | 1+ | B, P, B&W, W | Winter–Summer |
| Nemophila | <1 | B&W, B&Pur&W | Winter–Summer |
| Nepeta | 1-2 | L-B, L&W | Summer |
| Nicotiana alata | 2-3 | W | Summer |
| Oenothera | <1-3-1/2 | P, P-W, Y, W | Spring–Summer |
| Orthocarpus purpurascens | <1 | P-Pur&Y | Winter–Spring |
| Papaver | 1-1/2-5 | O, O-R, O-Y, P, R, W | Spring–Summer |
| Penstemon | 1-6 | L-R, O-R, P, P-R, P-W | Spring–Summer |
| Petalostemon purpureum | 3 | Pur&R | Summer |
| Phacelia | <1-2 | B, L | Spring |
| Phlox | <1-5 | L, P, P&W, R, W | Summer |
| Physostegia virginiana | 2-4 | L, P, W | Spring–Summer |
| Psilostrophe | 1-1/2-2 | Y | Spring–Summer |
| Ratibida columnifera | 1-1/2-3 | R&Y, Y | Summer |
| Romneya coulteri | 8 | W&Y | Summer–Fall |
| Rudbeckia hirta | 1-1/2-4+ | O-Y, Y | Summer–Fall |
| Salpiglossis sinuata | 1-3 | O-R, P, Pur, R, Y | Summer |
| Salvia | 1-3 | B, B-L, R | Spring–Summer |
| Silene | <1-2 | P, P-R, R | Spring–Summer |
| Sisyrinchium bellum | <1-1-1/2 | B&Y | Winter–Summer |
| Sphaeralcea | 3-4+ | L, O, O-R, P, R | Winter–Spring |
| Stachys coccinea | 1-2+ | R | Spring–Summer |
| Stylomecon heterophylla | 2 | O, Pur-R | Spring–Summer |
| Thalictrum | 2-6 | L, Pur, W | Spring–Summer |
| Tithonia rotundifolia | 2-6 | O-R, O-Y, Y | Summer–Fall |
| Venidium fastuosum | 2 | O, O-pur | Summer |
| Verbena | <1-2 | L, L-P, L-Pur, P, Pur | Winter–Fall |
| Viguiera | 3-6 | Y | Summer–Fall |
| Zinnia grandiflora | <1 | O-Y | Summer |

Color codes:
B=Blue G=green GF=gray foliage L=lavender O=orange
P=pink Pur=purple R=red W=white Y=yellow

Above: *Aquilegia caerulea,* Rocky Mountain columbine, is the state flower of Colorado and naturally well adapted to the Rocky Mountain region. Growth is exuberant, reaching 1-1/2 to 2 feet high.

Above right: *Aquilegia formosa,* scarlet columbine, is native to the pine forests of California. Flowers are abundant throughout summer; the red sepals and spurs create a bright contrast to the yellow flowers.

Right: *Achillea millefolium,* common yarrow, develops into a spreading, 1- to 3-foot plant topped by white, flat, flower clusters on a single stem. Flowers bloom in summer and fall.

## Achillea          Yarrow

Yarrow is a flowering perennial with aggressive roots and a carefree growth habit. It is excellent on slopes for erosion control. It also works well in the foreground of a mixed border and in meadow plantings. It is adaptable to all temperate areas of the West with a hardiness to about 0F. Once established, plants are low water users.

*A. filipendulina* 'Coronation Gold' is one of the tallest yarrows with bright yellow, flat-topped flowers in clusters on 3-foot plants. Native to Asia Minor. *A. millefolium,* common yarrow, develops into a spreading, 1- to 3-foot plant topped by white, flat, flower clusters on a single stem. Flowers bloom in summer and fall, with most profuse blooms from plants located in full sun. They can be used either fresh or dried in bouquets. 'Moonbeam' has pale yellow, flat flowerheads on 2-foot plants. 'Red Beauty' is pinkish red. Plants are strongly aromatic. Makes a fine lawn substitute. Native to Europe and western Asia.

*A. tomentosa,* woolly yarrow, grows to about 6 inches, developing into a ferny green mat. The yellow flowers stand well above the leaves. Use as a ground cover in sun or partial shade, in the border or rock garden. When used as a lawn substitute and after flowering, woolly yarrow can be mowed once each month in coastal and inland valley regions during summer to create a carpetlike cover. Use a nylon line trimmer or mower set to cut high.

**Planting & Care**—Sow seed or plant from containers in fall in mild regions; wait until spring in cold-winter areas. Sow seed on the soil surface; light is required to germinate seed. Grows best in light, not overly rich soil. If soil is too rich, foliage growth will be lush at the expense of the flowers. Keep soil moist until seedlings emerge and plants become established. As plants mature, they form clusters of underground roots that can be divided to extend plantings in late winter and early spring.

Native to Eurasia

Perennial; blooms spring to fall

Grows 6 to 36 inches high, spreads 18 to 24 inches wide

Provide with light, well-draining soil

Low to moderate water use

Plant in full sun along coast and inland valleys; provide afternoon shade in hot desert regions

Seeding rates: 1.5 grams per 100 sq. ft.; .25 ounce per 500 sq. ft.; 1 pound per acre

*Achillea millefolium*

## Aquilegia          Columbine

Columbines have a special fresh look, due in part to their fernlike foliage and tall erect flowers on long stems. They evoke a woodsy effect, effective in rock gardens and perennial borders. Hummingbirds are especially attracted to the flowers.

*A. caerulea,* Rocky Mountain columbine, is the state flower of Colorado and naturally well adapted to the Rocky Mountain region, and throughout most of the arid West. Growth is exuberant, reaching 1-1/2 to 2 feet high. Flowers are blue and white with 2-inch spurs on tall stems. *A. chrysantha,* golden-spurred columbine, is native to Arizona and New Mexico. It grows to 2-1/2 feet high, with clear yellow flowers 1-1/2 to 3 inches wide with spurs 2 to 2-1/2 inches long. *A. formosa,* scarlet columbine, is native to the pine forests of California. It grows to 2-1/2 feet high. Flowers are abundant throughout summer, the red sepals and spurs in bright contrast to the yellow flowers. Easy to grow.

*A. longissima,* yellow longspur columbine, is a favorite in its native Texas. 'Maxistar' grows 2 to 2-1/2 feet high and has large yellow flowers with long spurs. Prefers some shade and moderate moisture in summer.

**Planting & Care**—Before sowing seed in spring, place seed in a jar filled with sand and refrigerate for a month. This *cold-stratifies* the seed. Prepare soil so it is well-draining and high in organic matter to hold moisture. Sow seed on soil surface, but do not cover because seed needs light to germinate. Keep soil moist. New seedling growth may be slow; however, after plants develop, growth and flower production will be vigorous. Thin seedlings to 1 to 1-1/2 feet on center. After one growing season, cut back basal growth to just above the ground when plants go dormant in winter. Fresh, new growth will emerge the following spring. Problems with aphids and spider mites can occur in summer. Hose off minor infestations or spray with a soap-and-water solution.

Native to U.S. north temperate regions and western states

Perennial; blooms spring and summer

Grows 1-1/2 to 3 feet high with an equal to greater spread

Provide with well-draining, slightly acid soil

Moderate water use along coast; high water use in hot-summer regions

Plant in full sun along coast; provide morning sun, afternoon shade in hot-summer regions

Seeding rates: 8 grams per 100 sq. ft.; 2 ounces per 500 sq. ft.

*Aquilegia caerulea*

*Asclepias*
*tuberosa*

*Aster*
*bigelovii*

## Asclepias — Butterfly Weed

*Asclepias tuberosa*, butterfly weed, is aptly named because monarch butterflies like to swarm around the flowers. It also attracts hummingbirds, which makes it an excellent plant for the wildflower garden. The vivid orange, flat-topped flower clusters bloom on tall, 3-foot stems during late spring into late summer. After flowering, seed pods release small, silky, parachutelike seeds that float with the wind. Lance-shaped leaves 4 to 5 inches long crowd the tall stems to the base of flowers, giving the plant a sturdy appearance. Placing plants at the rear of low shrub borders or mixed perennial borders adds both color and foliage substance. Lesser-known *Asclepias* include:

*A. linaria*, pine-leaf milkweed, is native to Arizona. It has a typical milkweed growth habit with a woody base and thin, needlelike leaves. The clusters of white flowers in late spring and summer develop into inflated fruit pods in the fall. Plants become rounded, 3-foot subshrubs. Cold-hardy throughout the West.

*A. subulata*, desert milkweed, is a novel Arizona native. Stems are narrow, almost leafless. The 3-foot plants are enhanced with cream-colored summer flowers at the tips of the vertical stems. The flowers are followed by inflated pods that hold the seeds; plants reseed readily.

**Planting & Care**—Sow seed 1/8 inch deep in place in fall. Placing seed in the refrigerator for about two weeks prior to planting improves germination. Locate in full sun in porous, well-draining soil. Plants are low water users once they are established. Because of their deep taproots, plants are difficult to transplant. As plants age, more flowering stems are produced, which increases the color. Be patient, it might take several seasons before flowers are abundant. After plants have completed the bloom cycle and are dormant in the fall, cut back tall stems to basal growth for renewed growth in spring.

## Aster — Hardy Aster, Michaelmas Daisy

These charming flowers were once a standby in old-fashioned gardens. Asters are still one of the mainstays of the late-blooming perennial border, providing tumbling masses of color in August and September. Woody-based plants grow 2 to 4 feet high. Stalks must either be pinched back or staked. Secondary blooms can be encouraged by cutting off spent flowers. Asters are good in indoor bouquets.

*Aster bigelovii*, purple aster, is an annual or biennial that develops into a solid mound to 3 feet high. Lilac to burgundy flowers bloom in fall. Plants can be kept smaller by trimming back in late spring.

Perennial specialists are good sources for superior selections. Look for: *A. x frikartii* 'Wonder of Staffa' to 2-1/2 feet high. Lavender-blue flowers bloom from late spring to fall. Well adapted to coastal and inland valleys. Native to the Himalayas.

*A. novi-belgii* 'Crimson Brocade', 3 feet high, has semi-double crimson flowers.

Adapted to all regions. Not always readily available.

*A. tanacetifolius*, tahoka daisy, is an annual form that grows to 1-1/2 feet high. Flowers in shades of purple bloom midsummer to fall. Regular watering pays off with more flowers.

**Planting & Care**—The ideal method is to plant from containers in fall or spring. The common native asters can be grown from seed. Cold-stratify for two weeks in the refrigerator prior to planting. Thin to the best four or five well-spaced stalks in spring, pulling out weak and crowded ones. Pinch stems twice to induce bushiness, pinching off half the stalk each time. To lengthen the flowering time and to create a more informal appearance, don't pinch all the stems at once. Propagate cultivated varieties, *cultivars*, by dividing plants, or take cuttings in spring. A virus, aster yellows, is transmitted by leafhoppers and aphids. Plant resistant varieties.

## Baileya multiradiata — Desert Marigold

You'll often see a profusion of desert marigold in the Mojave Desert, in Arizona's Sonoran Desert and as far east as west Texas and north to Utah. This perennial provides an abundance of flowers over a long period and is often included in dry-climate seed mixes for this reason. Bloom is more profuse in regions with summer rains or with supplemental irrigation during summer. The basal leaf growth bears stems 6 to 18 inches long that produce bright yellow, daisylike flowers 1- to 1-3/4 inches in diameter. Reseeding occurs rapidly and volunteers increase the color show each season. Butterflies are attracted to the flowers.

Companion plants in the natural landscape include *Encelia farinosa*, brittlebush, *Ruellia peninsularis*, blue ruellia, *Fouquieria splendens*, ocotillo, *Opuntia* species and *Larrea tridentata*, creosote bush. All prefer similar, light, sandy soils and low moisture. Use on level land, on slopes and in natural landscaping among native or adapted plants.

**Planting & Care**—Sow seeds almost any time where you want plants to grow but best results will be with fall to spring seedings. Premoisten soil prior to applying seed. Sow 1/8 inch deep; rake soil lightly after seeding. After seedlings emerge (in 7 to 45 days), thin to 18 inches apart. Trim back spent flower stems and last year's growth in winter to stimulate new basal growth for the next season's blooms. Extra moisture may be required in fast-draining sandy soils or alluvial soils. Simulate summer rainfall by applying 1 inch of water monthly to encourage more growth and color.

Native to desert regions of U.S. Southwest

Perennial; blooms continuously spring through fall

Grows 1 to 1-1/2 feet high, spreads 1-1/2 to 2 feet wide

Provide with most any well-draining soil; prefers loose, deep, sandy soil

Low water use

Plant in full sun

Seeding rates: 5 grams per 100 sq. ft.; 1 ounce per 500 sq. ft.; 2 pounds per acre

*Baileya multiradiata*

## Berlandiera lyrata — Chocolate Flower, Green Eyes

Chocolate flower produces a fascinating fragrance similar to that of chocolate. The flowering season extends from spring into summer. Plants are perennial and grow to 1-1/2 feet high, producing cheerful sprays of flowers in shades of yellow, the undersides of petals streaked with bright red veins. Green *bracts*, modified leaves, remain after petals fall. These are decorative and can be used in dried arrangements.

Flower heads expand in the morning hours, then droop in the afternoon heat. Leaves to 7 inches long are green above and whitish underneath. These colors make them compatible with other gray-leaved plants such as *Salvia farinacea*, blue salvia, and *Aster* species. Flowers also attract butterflies.

To best appreciate the unique fragrance, sow seed in clusters near walks or outdoor living areas. Plant companion wildflowers *Eustoma grandiflorum*, Texas bluebells, and *Coreopsis* species in the foreground.

**Planting & Care**—Sow seed 1/8 inch deep in place in the fall or spring, tamping lightly into the soil surface. Keep soil moist. Seeds germinate in one to three months when temperatures are in the 60F to 70F range. Plants accept full sun but are best with partial shade in hottest areas. Mature spread in well-prepared soil is to 2-1/2 feet; thin seedlings accordingly to allow for uncrowded growth. Chocolate flower accepts low water after plants are well established. Deadhead spent flowers as you notice them to stimulate new growth and to strengthen stems.

Native to Kansas, Arkansas to Arizona and northern Mexico

Perennial; blooms spring into summer

Grows to 1-1/2 feet high, spreads 2 to 2-1/2 feet wide

Prefers well-draining soil

Low water use

Plant in full sun, partial shade best in hot climates

Seeding rates: 10 grams per 100 sq. ft.; 3 ounces per 500 sq. ft.; 5 pounds per acre

*Berlandiera lyrata*

*Asclepias tuberosa,* butterfly weed, is aptly named because monarch butterflies like to swarm around the flowers. It also attracts hummingbirds. The vivid orange, flat-topped flower clusters bloom on tall stems during late spring into late summer.

*Aster tanacetifolius,* tahoka daisy, is an annual aster that grows to 1-1/2 feet high. Flowers in shades of purple bloom midsummer to fall.

*Berlandiera lyrata,* chocolate flower, produces a fascinating fragrance similar to that of chocolate. Plants are perennial and grow to 1-1/2 feet high, producing sprays of flowers in shades of yellow.

*Baileya multiradiata,* desert marigold, is a perennial that provides an abundance of flowers over a long period and is often included in dry-climate seed mixes for this reason. Here it makes an attractive combination with *Penstemon parryi.*

*Gallery of Wildflowers* ■ 45

*Brachycome iberidifolia*

## Brachycome iberidifolia — Swan River Daisy

This is a favorite annual for close-up viewing. Plants develop into multi-branched, mounding clumps to 1 foot high, spreading 1-1/2 feet wide. During spring and summer, blue, white or pink daisies to 1 inch wide cover the plant. The finely divided leaves are 8 inches long yet are often hidden by the profuse flowers.

Swan River daisy can be used in flower beds as an edging and is particularly charming in window boxes and containers. The mounding growth also provides an interesting effect in rock gardens as plants flow neatly over and around boulders. Plants are well behaved and require little maintenance.

Swan River daisy is native to Australia and adaptable to all areas as long as seed is sown after frost. Blends well with white, rose or purple *Lobularia maritima*, sweet alyssum, as a border, or with *Catharanthus roseus*, periwinkle, in the background.

*B. multifida* is a perennial companion plant. Plants are grown from cuttings and set out after danger of frost has passed. Flower colors are predominantly shades of blue.

**Planting & Care**—Plants are easy to grow from seed. Sow in place 1/8 inch deep in well-prepared and well-draining soil where plants are to be located. Sow after all danger of frost has passed in spring. Thin seedlings 1 to 1-1/2 feet apart after they reach 2 to 3 inches high to allow for plants to develop properly. Provide with deep, regular irrigations. If soil is heavy clay or caliche, be careful not to overwater plants. In desert and hot inland areas, locate plants where they will receive filtered or afternoon shade. Plants will accept full sun along the coast.

*Campanula rotundifolia*

## Campanula — Bellflower

*Campanula* species are attractive perennial plants well suited for close-up viewing. Selecting a bellflower for the landscape is not difficult because there are over 300 species available. They are suitable in rock gardens, containers, hanging baskets, mixed borders, around fountains and pools and as a spreading ground cover in the shade.

*C. isophylla*, star-of-Bethlehem, is native to Italy. It is excellent in a hanging basket. 'Alba' has white flowers; 'Caerulea' has blue flowers. *C. persicifolia*, peach-leaved bluebell, bears blue, white or pink flowers. Plants grow 2 to 3 feet high. *C. poscharskyana*, Serbian bellflower, is a perennial that prefers well-draining, highly organic soil, regular moisture and filtered shade, which makes it excellent for a mini-oasis. Plants accept slightly more sun in coastal areas. Sprays of star-shaped, 1-inch, lavender flowers bloom from spring into early summer on vigorous, spreading, multi-branched plants to 1 foot high. Long, heart-shaped, light green leaves are irregularly toothed.
*C. pyramidalis*, chimney bellflower, grows 4 to 6 feet high with blue or white flowers.
*C. rotundifolia*, harebell, bluebells of Scotland, grows as a mat-forming carpet to 20 inches high. Bell-shaped flowers are lavender-blue.

**Planting & Care**—Sow seed on the soil surface in spring. When temperatures are in the 60F to 70F range, seedlings will appear in two to three weeks. Many selections are also available in containers at nurseries. Grow in full sun along the coast; provide afternoon shade or dappled shade of deciduous trees in hot climates. Provide additional water if planted with shrubs or other plants. Also requires more water in summer. As plants age, divide to increase plantings. Slugs and snails sometimes bother low-growing forms.

## Castilleja        Paintbrush

Paintbrushes are spectacular plants but a challenge to grow, either from seed or as transplants. It is believed they benefit from being grown with grasses and parasitize the grass roots. Experiments indicate they may not require it, but germination and establishment are improved. Most paintbrushes do best at 2,000 to 4,000 feet.

*Castilleja californica* is an annual that grows to 2-1/2 feet high with scarlet-tipped *bracts*—modified leaves that look like flowers. It is adapted to coastal California south to northern Baja California.
*C. chromosa*, desert paintbrush, is the most prolific paintbrush in the West. It is found in California's Mojave Desert, and in New Mexico and Wyoming. It is perennial, producing orange-red flowers and bracts during July to September.
*C. indivisa*, Texas paintbrush, is an annual or biennial species that produces one of the brightest of the paintbrush flowers. Terminal spikes on 15-inch stems include both striking red flowers and leaflike bracts. Flowering season extends from March to June. Adapted to a wide range in eastern Texas. Its natural habitat is along roadsides in damp soil.
*C. integra* produces brilliant orange-red flowers during spring and summer. Plants grow to 16 inches high. It is best adapted to higher-elevation climates, such as the Rocky Mountain region.
*C. purpurea*, purple paintbrush, is an annual or perennial native to Texas. Flowers also come in pink, yellow and orange. Include in small rock gardens or in meadow plantings. Grows best in sandy or limestone soils in full sun or partial shade.

**Planting & Care**—Indian paintbrush species can be a real challenge to grow from seed. Cold-stratification (see page 118) is believed to speed up germination. Sow 1/8 inch deep where plants are to grow. Seedlings seem to germinate better when sowed with gramagrass and in association with pine trees. The deep taproot makes transplanting difficult.

*Castilleja chromosa*

## Centaurea cyanus      Bachelor's-Button, Cornflower

This hardy annual is originally from Europe and the Near East. After being planted in gardens in the eastern United States, bachelor's-button escaped cultivation and has now naturalized. You can see it blooming during spring and summer along roadsides and meadows east of the Rocky Mountains.

Bachelor's-button is an excellent choice in dry-climate gardens because of its low water requirement. Plants also thrive in flower beds that receive regular moisture. Brilliant, ruffled, sapphire-blue daisy flowers cover plants that grow to 1 to 3 feet high. 'Alba' has white flowers. Leaves are gray-green and 2 to 3 inches long. The flowering period begins in late spring and lasts through summer.

Place bachelor's-button in the back of the border with yellow-flowering annuals and perennials such as chrysanthemums. It is also an attractive container plant. Use cut flowers for old-fashioned bouquets.

The 'Polka Dot' strain, a dwarf 16 inches high, is available in blue, red, pink, rose, white and wine-red flower colors. Flowers have best appearance in cool weather. An attractive, low-water-use companion is *C. gymnocarpa*, dusty-miller. The blue flowers of bachelor's-button contrast nicely with dusty-miller's gray leaves and yellow flowers.

**Planting & Care**—Seeds germinate readily. Plant in place in fall in mild-winter regions, in spring in cold-winter regions. Sow seeds 1/8 inch deep, being sure they are completely covered to provide the total darkness required for germination. Locate in full sun. Prefers light, sterile, well-draining soils. Thin seedlings to 2 feet apart to allow for spread. Set out container-grown plants in the spring or fall in coastal areas, in spring in inland valleys, and in early spring in desert areas.

*Centaurea cyanus*

Above: *Campanula rotundifolia,* bluebells of Scotland, grows as a mat-forming carpet to 20 inches high. Use in rock gardens, containers, hanging baskets, around fountains and pools and as a ground cover in the shade.

Above right: *Castilleja integra* produces brilliant orange-red flowers during spring and summer. Plants grow to 1-1/2 feet high. It is well adapted to higher elevation climates.

Right: *Brachycome iberidifolia,* Swan River daisy, develops into a multibranched, mounding clump to 1 foot high, spreading 1-1/2 feet wide. Blue, white or pink daisies cover the plant during spring and summer.

Far left: *Centaurea cyanus,* bachelor's-button, has a long flowering period, lasting from late spring through summer.

Left: *Cerastium tomentosum,* snow-in-summer, makes an effective accent plant or small-area ground cover.

Below left: *Chrysanthemum carinatum,* summer chrysanthemum, produces daisylike flowers to 2 inches across.

Below: *Clarkia amoena whitneyi,* farewell-to-spring, blooms late in spring just as summer begins to arrive.

—

Perennial; blooms late spring and summer

—

Grows 6 to 8 inches high, spreads 2 to 3 feet wide

—

Provide with well-draining soil

—

Low water use

—

Plant in full sun along coast; provide afternoon shade in hot-summer regions

—

Seeding rates: 3 grams per 100 sq. ft.; .5 ounces per 500 sq. ft.

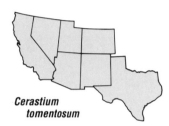

*Cerastium tomentosum*

Native to Morocco

—

Annual and perennial; varied bloom periods; see text

—

Grows 1-1/2 to 2-1/2 feet high, spreads 2 to 3 feet wide

—

Provide with well-draining soil improved with organic matter

—

Moderate water use depending on temperature range

—

Plant in full sun along the coast; in partial shade in hot-summer regions

—

Seeding rates: .07 grams per 100 sq. ft.; 1.5 ounces per 500 sq. ft.; 6 to 8 pounds per acre

*Chrysanthemum maximum*

## Cerastium tomentosum — Snow-in-Summer

The low, neat, woolly leaves of snow-in-summer create a silvery carpet for its small, white flowers that bloom during spring and summer. This is an exceptional flowering perennial ground cover with many landscape uses: bordering walks, as a solid pattern, small-area ground cover, flower bed borders, low pattern planting among perennials, cascading from a terrace and in rock gardens and foreground to shrub beds. Plants grow only 8 inches high but spread as much as 2 to 3 feet wide.

Adapted to all climate zones when given plenty of sun and planted in soil with good drainage. Afternoon shade in hot-summer climates is recommended. The best plants for combination plantings are dark-leaved plants such as *Lavandula*, lavender, *Gaillardia*, blanketflower, *Brachycome iberidfolia*, Swan River daisy, and *Festuca* species, blue fescue. Plants can become aggressive and overrun planting areas. There is a dormant period in cold weather, but plants recover as temperatures warm in spring.

**Planting & Care**—Sow seed 1/16 inch deep in place during spring, tamping soil firmly. Seeds germinate in two weeks and growth is rapid. Overwatering can cause problems with rot, so soil drainage is important. Water in the morning rather than evening so moisture will not remain on leaves overnight. Planting on well-draining slopes or mounds is ideal. Snow-in-summer is also often available in flats as transplants. Avoid purchasing plants in flats that have become overgrown because the roots can be difficult to separate for transplanting. Trim off spent flowers with a nylon line trimmer or hedge shears to keep plant looking neat. As plants age, reseed or replant beds to fill in bare spots.

## Chrysanthemum — Chrysanthemum

The chrysanthemum originated in China and for many centuries has been a favored plant in that country, as well as in Japan and Korea. The genus is huge, providing gardeners with many important garden plants. Once established, mums are moderate-water-use plants. With fall-blooming mums, grow varieties adapted to your climate so plants have the opportunity to attain full bloom before frost.

*Chrysanthemum carinatum*, summer chrysanthemum, grows 18 to 30 inches high with an equal spread. It is normally a summer- to fall-flowering annual, but plants will flower in late winter and spring in mild-winter regions. A wide range of colors are available—white, yellow, rose, salmon, scarlet, orange and purple. The center is dark, surrounded with contrasting color bands. Cut flowers are long-lasting. Use in borders with low-growing annuals in the foreground. Best adapted to coastal areas. (It has escaped to naturalize throughout the San Diego region.)

*C. frutescens*, marguerite, is a short-lived perennial or annual producing attractive yellow and white daisies. They grow vigorously 3 to 4 feet high, blooming in spring and summer. The bloom season is practically year-round along the coast. In regions with high heat the flowering season comes to an end as early as June. *C. maximum (C. x superbum)* is the popular Shasta daisy. It is a perennial available in a variety of forms. Favorites include the double white 'Ester Reed'; 'Alaska', with large white single flowers; and 'Majestic', with large, white, single flowers with yellow centers.

**Planting & Care**—In cold-winter areas, sow seed 1/16 inch deep in spring. In mild-winter areas, sow in fall. Seedlings and container plants are available at nurseries. Locate in full sun. Accepts almost any soil. Water requirement is moderate; more water is needed in desert areas. Plants reseed readily. Divide clumps of Shasta daisy every year or two.

## Clarkia — Farewell-to-Spring, Satin Flower

*Clarkia amoena whitneyi*, farewell-to-spring, is one of the most cheerful annuals to enhance a garden border or wildflower mix. The pale pink or lavender flowers of this California native bloom late in spring as the first touch of summer begins to arrive. Plant stems grow 1 to 2 feet high, topped with 2-inch, fan-shaped flowers that are usually pink with dark red spots on each petal. Farewell-to-spring works well in the background, the colors blending well with borders of blue pansies, cornflower, phlox and purple or white sweet alyssum. When cutting the long-lasting flowers for indoor arrangements, make branch cuts just as the top flower bud begins to open.

*C. concinna*, red-ribbons, is a native California annual that grows 8 to 16 inches high. Flowers come in rich pink and lavender hues. The form is unusual, with pendulous buds that open with 1-inch petals twice as long as the width, accented with flattened filaments. Rounded 1/2- to 2-inch green leaves are overshadowed by the brilliant flowers that bloom in spring and last until early summer.

*C. pulchella*, deerhorn clarkia, is native to an area that stretches from the Rocky Mountains to the Pacific Coast. Growth is erect 8 to 18 inches high. Flowers are bright pink to lavender.

*C. unguiculata*, mountain garland (also known as *C. elegans*), produces flowers in rose, purple, white, salmon, pink and orange during late spring to early summer. It grows 2 to 3 feet high. It is best adapted to areas where rainfall is more abundant.

**Planting & Care**—In mild-winter regions, sow seed in fall; in cold-winter regions sow seed in spring. Sow 1/16 inch deep where you want plants to grow because seedlings are difficult to transplant. Plants do reseed readily, however. Provide moderate moisture after seeding and until flowers begin developing. In warm areas, supply supplemental irrigation during dry spells to increase production of flowers.

Native to California and the Pacific Northwest

Annual; blooms late spring to early summer

Grows 8 inches to 3 feet high, spreads 1-1/2 to 3 feet wide

Provide with well-draining soils; accepts sandy soils

Moderate water use

Plant in sun or partial shade

Seeding rates: 3 grams per 100 sq. ft.; .5 ounces per 500 sq. ft.; 2 pounds per acre

*Clarkia amoena whitneyi*

## Consolida ambigua — Annual Larkspur

Annual larkspur is similar to the perennial delphinium but develops more vigorous growth in a wider range of colors. Flowers, many of them double, are profuse during spring and early summer. Strong vertical flower spikes reach 3 to 4 feet high, creating a strong accent. The 1- to 1-1/2-inch flowers are available in white and shades of blue, pink, rose, salmon and red and are cherished by hummingbirds. Foliage is deeply cut, which creates a refined effect along stems.

Annual larkspur is well adapted to high-temperature regions in the arid West. Use it in sunny locations in the background of natural borders. Because of the height of its flower spikes, locate plants in groups for vertical design elements and to help protect them from the wind. *Alstroemeria* and yellow or white marguerites, *Chrysanthemum*, are colorful companion plants. Larkspur is also attractive in indoor flower arrangements.

**Planting & Care**—Sow seed in place during fall months where plants are to grow. Cover seed with at least 1/8 inch of soil for germination. After seedlings reach 3 to 6 inches high thin plants 1 to 1-1/2 feet apart. Some strains such as Giant Imperial, Steeplechase and Regal develop more basal branches so they require even more space for spread. Prefers well-draining soil. Moderate water at regular intervals is important. Accepts full sun but does best with afternoon shade in hot-summer areas. After the first period of bloom has passed, cut back old flower stems to encourage a second bloom. This is more likely to occur in cooler climates.

Native to southern Europe and the Mediterranean region

Annual; blooms during spring in hot-summer regions, during early summer in cooler areas

Grows 3 to 4 feet high, spreads to 1 foot or more wide

Provide with well-draining soil improved with organic matter

Moderate deep water at regular intervals

Plant in full sun

Seeding rates: 12 grams per 100 sq. ft.; 4 ounces per 500 sq. ft.; 10 pounds per acre

*Consolida ambigua*

Right: *Cosmos bipinnatus,* cosmos, is native to Mexico and well adapted throughout the Southwest. When given a sunny spot its bloom period can last through summer and into fall.

Below: *Coreopsis* species provide long-lasting color even in hot, dry conditions.

Below right: *Clarkia unguiculata,* mountain garland, is a late-spring to early summer bloomer. It is common in the Coast Ranges and Sierra Nevada foothills in California.

# Coreopsis

### Coreopsis, Tickseed

*Coreopsis* is a star performer with many uses in the landscape. It is ideal for a natural garden, on slopes, in wildflower mixes and to blend with background shrubs in wide garden borders. Butterflies are attracted to the bright flower colors. Cut flowers are long-lasting for indoor bouquets.

*C. auriculata* is a perennial native to the southeastern U.S. Plants grow 1-1/2 feet high with single, yellow, 1-1/2- to 2-inch flowers. 'Nana' grows to a compact 6 inches high, spreading up to 2 feet wide.

*C. bigelovii* is well adapted throughout the Southwest. It grows to 2 feet high with flowers almost 2 inches across that bloom early spring to early summer.

*C. lanceolata*, also a perennial, is an important ingredient in wildflower mixes, flowering through spring in sunny locations. It often has an encore performance in early fall. Bright yellow, 1- to 2-inch, daisylike flowers have attractive jagged edges. Plants grow 2 to 3 feet high with heavy foliage growth; basal leaves reach 3 to 6 inches long. Plants self-sow profusely and can be invasive.

*C. tinctoria*, plains coreopsis, is an annual that grows to 3 feet high with a 2-foot spread. It is a useful addition to wildflower mixes or planted in masses. The striking mahogany red and yellow flowers are abundant in late spring to early summer. 'Dwarf' has the same characteristics, except it reaches a height and spread of 1-1/2 feet.

**Planting & Care**—Sow seed on soil surface in place in fall in warm regions, covering seed with a thin layer of soil. Seedlings germinate within one to two weeks. To achieve earlier blooms in cold areas, sow indoors in flats and transplant seedlings outdoors after danger of frost has passed. Plants can withstand short periods of dry conditions as well as prolonged moisture. In hottest areas, increase moisture to extend bloom period. Remove spent flower stems to promote additional blooms. In late fall cut back to basal growth and divide plants to increase plantings.

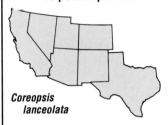

*Coreopsis lanceolata*

# Cosmos

### Cosmos

*Cosmos bipinnatus*, pink cosmos, is native to Mexico and well adapted throughout the Southwest. It is a much-loved garden annual that is quite colorful when given a sunny spot. It was common in mission gardens and hacienda courtyards of Mexico and California in the early 1800s.

The plant height of 7 feet or more and equal spread creates an outstanding backdrop in wide borders, against fences or as a filler among large shrubs. Growth is rapid, providing airy, soft-foliaged filler in a new garden until slower-growing trees, shrubs and perennials develop some size. Flowers are good for bouquets if cut when they have just opened. Divided leaves, almost fernlike in texture, combine with large, daisylike flowers 2 to 3 inches across. Flower colors vary from soft pink, rose-red and deep crimson to pure white. Bloom period is long, lasting through summer and into fall.

Many improved selections are available in colors that range from rose to lavender, purple and crimson. 'Sunny Red' is available as seed or as container plants at nurseries. It is heat tolerant and grows to 1 foot high with rich vermilion blooms.

*C. sulphureus* is similar to *C. bipinnatus*, but grows to 3 feet high. Locate plants where they'll receive protection from strong winds. Also water deeply to develop a strong, deep root system. Flowers are bright red, orange and gold in single, double or semidouble forms.

**Planting & Care**—Sow seed 1/8 inch deep in place spring to summer, or set out plants from containers. Seeds sprout within a week or so when soil temperatures are 65F to 75F. Flowers follow within two months. Plant in light sandy or sterile soil. If the soil is too rich, you'll have more leaves and fewer flowers. Cosmos are relatively water-efficient plants. Add an organic mulch around the root zone to help keep the soil moist. Plants reseed readily and attract birds.

*Cosmos bipinnatus*

**Delphinium
cardinale**

**Dianthus
deltoides**

## Delphinium                    Scarlet Larkspur

*Delphinium cardinale*, scarlet larkspur, is a delightful perennial and a reddish scarlet alternative to the usual blue *Delphinium* species. Flowers are actually a combination of scarlet and yellow and grow to 1 inch long. Spikes 3 to 6 feet high are covered with the brilliantly colored flowers from late spring to early summer. Leaves on stalks 3 to 9 inches wide are deeply lobed. Because basal leaves wither early in the season, by the time the plant blooms it is mostly a long, leafless panicle of spurred red flowers.

Locate in background areas in clusters combined with *Linaria vulgaris,* butter and eggs, which acts as a screen for the leafless stalks. Also excellent as a colorful cut flower. Flowers are a special attraction to hummingbirds. Although native to central California's coastal mountains, plants are adapted to grow from British Columbia to Southern California, and are common in the San Gabriel Mountains.

*D. ajacis*, rocket larkspur (also known as *Consolida ambigua*), grows 3 to 4 feet high and 1 foot wide. Flower spikes in mixed colors bloom on top of deeply cut foliage. After flowering season is complete, remove spent plants. Well adapted to Southwest climates.

**Planting & Care**—Plant seed of scarlet larkspur in place in early spring. Plant seed of rocket larkspur in fall. If you harvest seed in cold climates, place in airtight containers and refrigerate until time to plant in spring. Cover seed with at least 1/16 to 1/8 inch of soil. Locate in sun or partial shade, and provide with porous, organic-rich soil and moderate water. If your soil is acid, add lime. Plants develop deep roots and require deep irrigation.

## Dianthus                    Maiden Pink, Sweet William

*Dianthus barbatus*, sweet William, is adapted throughout the United States and is grown as a perennial or annual. The grassy leaves form clumps 10 to 20 inches high. The carnationlike flowers are 3/4 inch in diameter and produce a scent similar to cloves. They come in pink, rose, red, purple and bicolors. Flowers bloom in spring and again in the fall as temperatures cool.

*D. deltoides*, maiden pink, is a vigorous perennial, staying low to the ground to produce a matlike cover. Flowers are 3/4 inch long, deep pink with dark rings around the centers; edges are toothed. Flower stems reach 8 to 12 inches high and are covered with small leaves. Flowers bloom during summer and again in the fall. Landscape uses include rock gardens, flower borders or small foreground patterns that create a grasslike effect.

Many other perennial *Dianthus* species are available in containers or as seed at nurseries. Their special colors, fragrance and low growth make them versatile plants for home gardens.

**Planting & Care**—Sow seed in place 1/8 inch deep in the fall or spring. Plants develop rapidly, but flowering is more profuse the second season. In hot-summer areas, plant where they'll receive afternoon shade. Along the coast, locate in full sun. Provide with well-draining fertile soil and regular moisture but do not overwater. *D. deltoides* generally requires less water than *D. barbatus*. Shear off spent flowers for a clean look and to encourage new growth and flowers. Existing plants can also be propagated by division.

# Digitalis purpurea

**Common Foxglove**

Foxglove is a bold perennial or biennial background plant that produces 4-foot, vertical spikes laden with purple flowers. The flowers are so striking they tend to dominate a garden scene. Arrange in groups of three to five in a triangular pattern for accent planting. Bloom period lasts for a long period from spring to fall. The 2- to 3-inch, pendulous blossoms are arranged in heavy clusters along the stems and are highly attractive to hummingbirds. The rough-textured, woolly, gray-green leaves form strong basal growth. Smaller leaves at the top of the stalks are known as a source for the medicinal drug digitalis.

**Planting & Care**  For best results, prepare soil well in advance, mixing in large quantities of organic matter. The goal is to create an environment similar to a shaded forest floor. Sow seed in fall on soil surface. Keep soil evenly moist. Plants will bloom the following year. Spring seeding is also possible, but flowering will be light until the next season. For earlier flowers start with container-grown plants purchased from the nursery. Space plants at least 3 feet apart to avoid crowding. As in seeding, soil should be rich in organic matter to retain moisture. After first flowers have completed their bloom cycle, cut back main branches. Side branches will grow to produce another bloom cycle. Plants reseed freely after flowering but generally revert to white flower colors. May need to control slugs and snails.

Native to Portugal and Spain

Biennial; blooms early summer to fall

Grows 2 to 4 feet high or more, spreads 2 to 4 feet wide

Provide with well-draining soil enriched with organic blend

Moderate to high water use

Plant in partial shade along the coast; in partial to full shade in hot climates

Seeding rates: 1.5 grams per 100 sq. ft.; .25 ounces per 500 sq. ft.; 1/2 pound per acre

*Digitalis purpurea*

# Dimorphotheca sinuata

**African Daisy**

(Also known as *Dimorphotheca aurantiaca*.)

African daisy is a common, easy-to-grow annual wildflower that has proven it is at home in warm, dry climates. The bright apricot, yellow and orange flowers bloom profusely in early spring, lasting until warm weather comes on.

African daisy is one of the most effective wildflowers in creating a fast, colorful carpeting effect. It also creates a quick, temporary slope cover for erosion control. Other landscape uses include parking strip plantings and narrow, nook-and-cranny planting beds. Plants grow to about 1 foot high, with leaves 2 to 3 inches long. Flowers reach up to 2 inches in diameter but are often smaller. In low-elevation desert climates, the flowering season begins as early as late February and extends to April. In cold-winter climates, flowers bloom from May to August. Flowers close on cloudy days and at night.

*D. pluvialis* 'Glisting White', white African daisy, produces flowers that have an attractive sparkling quality. Plant in full sun. Water need is low to moderate.

**Planting & Care**—One of the secrets of growing this South African annual is to premoisten the seedbed. Apply water slowly until it reaches a depth of 6 inches. The soil will then contain adequate moisture for the fast-growing seedlings. After seedlings develop their initial leaves and if temperatures are warm, an additional deep watering simulating a slow, steady rainfall will bring plants into their flowering period. Plant seed in early fall to early winter. Grows best in light, well-draining soils; accepts alkaline or sterile soils. Seeds are large and need a minimum of 1/4 to 1/2 inch of soil cover. Don't overseed or seedlings will shade out each other, causing growth to be weak. Locate in full sun. After flowering, allow plants to go to seed.

Native to South Africa

Annual; blooms early spring to early summer

Grows to 1 foot high, spreads 6 to 12 inches wide

Provide with light, well-draining soil; accepts alkaline and sterile soils

Low water use

Plant in full sun—important

Seeding rates: 10 grams per 100 sq. ft.; 3 ounces per 500 sq. ft.; 8 pounds per acre

*Dimorphotheca sinuata*

Right: *Clarkia amoena whitneyi,* farewell to spring, backlit by the sun.

Below: *Cosmos bipinnatus,* cosmos, is fast growing, and often used as a filler plant until permanent landscape trees and shrubs produce substance.

Far left: *Digitalis purpurea*, common foxglove, is a bold perennial or biennial background plant. Flowers are so striking they tend to dominate a garden scene.

Left: *Delphinium cardinale*, scarlet larkspur, produce flowers that are actually a combination of scarlet and yellow. Spikes 3 to 6 feet high are covered with the brilliantly colored flowers from May to June.

*Dimorphotheca sinuata*, African daisy, is a common, easy-to-grow annual wildflower that has proven it is at home in warm, dry climates. The bright apricot, yellow and orange flowers bloom profusely in early spring, lasting until warm weather comes on.

*Dyssodia
tenuiloba*

*Echinacea
purpurea*

## Dyssodia tenuiloba — Golden Fleece

*Dyssodia tenuiloba* is a valued and delightful miniature annual. Its dwarfish size, to 1 foot high, and miniature 1-inch yellow flowers are well suited to small-space locations, especially in situations where you can view the plants close up. Pinnately parted leaves, almost threadlike, are green and lush enough to provide a background for the small flowers.

Tuck plants or sow seeds in and among crevices in rock gardens or plant in masses on mounds among boulders, which will provide a cool, moist environment for root growth. Plant in clumps at the base of *Felicia amelloides*, blue marguerite, for a delightful color combination, or with *Salvia farinacea*, mealy cup sage, with its velvety blue flowers. The flowering period of golden fleece extends from early summer into fall, long after the majority of spring annuals have completed their cycle of bloom. In mild-winter areas, plants may persist as perennials and reseed vigorously in loose dry soil.

*D. pentachaeta*, golden dyssodia, grows to just 6 inches high, covered with a brilliant mass of yellow flowers. Flowers are most prolific in spring, but bloom period can be extended with irrigation. Plants accept poor soil and a location in full sun. Native to the Southwest, from west Texas to southern Arizona.

**Planting & Care**—Sow seed on soil surface in flats for transplanting or where you want plants to grow. Some nurseries in dry-climate regions carry plants in containers during fall. Sandy or loam soil is preferred and should be well draining. Plants develop flowers approximately four months from seeding. Locate plants in full sun for best results, but avoid reflected sun of western exposures. Established plants normally require less water than most annual bedding plants.

## Echinacea — Purple Coneflower

The unusual plum-pink color and stature of *Echinacea purpurea*, purple coneflower, attracts attention in the landscape, especially when used against a backdrop of a plain wall or fence. Including it with drifts of other tall-growing perennials or annuals such as *Cosmos* or *Helianthus*, sunflower, creates an even more dramatic effect. This perennial is a robust and agressive grower and even competes well with grasses. It reaches 3 to 5 feet high so is best used in background plantings as described above. Flowers bloom summer to fall.

*E. angustifolia*, black Samson, is well adapted to the Southwest. The unique, plum-pink flowers have darker purple centers, the petals turning into a draped position. Flowers are 4 inches across on stems that stand well above the coarse, 3- to 8-inch, oblong leaves.

**Planting & Care**—If seeds are planted in early spring, seedlings will appear in 15 to 30 days. Sow seed 1/8 inch deep. Flowers sometimes develop by

fall. Locate in a sunny area in well-prepared soil. Once established, water requirements are low. In low-elevation, hot-summer gardens and in fast-draining soils, increase water use from low to moderate. After the flowering season is complete, cut back tall stems to near ground level. Leave plants in place to regrow the following spring or divide and transplant to new locations in the garden.

# Encelia

## Brittle Bush, Encienso

*Encelia farinosa*, brittle bush, is one of the Southwest desert's most widely distributed native flowering plants. It can be seen throughout low-elevation desert areas of California and Arizona and mid-elevation regions of south-eastern Nevada—wherever temperatures do not fall below 30F for too long a period. It is almost herbaceous in character, with a growth pattern that ebbs and flows according to how much rainfall or irrigation plants receive. Flowering is most profuse mid-March through April but can begin as early as November in frost-free areas. Yellow flowers on tall, 12-inch stalks can cover the 3- to 4-foot, gray, mounding plant with bouquets of blooms.

*E. californica*, California encelia, has similar characteristics, but growth is more open. It is well adapted to the coast and foothills of the coastal ranges.

Brittle bush blends with plants in the natural garden that have similar moisture needs. For naturalized combinations, include with *Salvia greggii*, red salvia, *Hesperaloe* and *Tagetes* species. Use California encelia in combination with *Salvia clevelandii*, *Artemisia* and *Lavandula* species.

**Planting & Care**—Easy to start from seed when planted in place during fall or early spring. Brittle bush is also included in wildflower mixes. Container plants are commonly available and can be planted at any season, but fall is ideal. With time, landscape plants often develop heavy woody branches. Thin and cut back soft branches at least one-third, maintaining natural form, for renewed growth after flowering. After shearing, selectively thin inside branches to allow sunlight into the plant's interior. Plants have low to moderate water requirements, and when water is abundant plants can become weak and straggly. Black aphids also tend to attack such plants.

*Encelia farinosa*

# Eschscholzia

## California Poppy

*Eschscholzia californica*, California poppy, is one of the most popular of all wildflowers and is the state flower of the Golden State. From foggy coastal slopes to inland valleys and desert sand dunes, the satiny, bright to deep orange or yellow flowers put on a spectacular show of color from spring into early summer. Blue-green, finely divided foliage grows in graceful mounds with 2-inch flowers atop 12- to 18-inch stems. Seed growers have developed strains that are orange to pink in color, but most gardeners prefer the natural colors of the species.

*E. caespitosa*, dwarf California poppy, foothill poppy, is a more compact annual form than *E. californica*, developing densely tufted growth to 9 inches high. Bright yellow, single, 1-inch flowers are supported on leafless flower stalks.
*E. mexicana*, Mexican gold poppy, is the most popular annual wildflower in Arizona and west Texas. Appearance is very similar to California poppy, except flower color tends to be more yellow rather than deep orange, and plants are slightly smaller. On plains and mountain slopes below 4,500 feet, blooming begins in mid-February in warmer areas such as Phoenix and Yuma, and in March and April in areas around Picacho Peak northwest of Tucson.

Landscape and garden uses for these poppies include meadows, slopes, rock gardens, natural gardens and flower beds. Often included in wildflower mixes. Flowers close at night and in cloudy weather.

**Planting & Care**—Sow seed 1/16 inch deep in place in prepared soil in fall. Moisten soil to 12 inches deep before seeding. Seedlings will appear in 15 to 30 days. Thin seedlings 1 to 1-1/2 feet apart to allow plants to develop. Tolerant of low water, but supplying moderate moisture increases flowering. Cut off old flower stems as you notice them to promote additional flowering. Plants adapt well to sunny locations in a wide range of soils, establish easily and reseed reliably.

*Eschscholzia californica*

Above: *Echinacea purpurea,* purple coneflower, attracts attention in the landscape. It reaches 3 feet high or more so is best used in background plantings. Flowers bloom summer to fall.

Above right: *Eschscholzia californica,* California poppy, works well in natural landscape plantings.

Right: *Encelia farinosa,* brittle bush, produces profuse numbers of yellow flowers on tall, 12-inch stalks. Here it combines with *Penstemon parryi.*

*Eschscholzia californica,* California poppy, is a spectacular wildflower in nature (above left), and in home garden settings (above). The satiny, bright to deep orange or yellow flowers put on a show of color from spring into early summer.

*Eschscholzia mexicana,* Mexican gold poppy, is the most popular annual wildflower in Arizona and west Texas. It is very similar to California poppy, except flowers tend to be more golden or yellow rather than deep orange. Plants are often slightly smaller.

*Euphorbia marginata*

*Eustoma grandiflorum*

## Euphorbia — Snow-on-the-Mountain

The unusual foliage of *Euphorbia marginata*, snow-on-the-mountain, provides contrast and interest in flower beds and as single specimens for close-up viewing. Oval, light green leaves are striped and margined in white with the upper surface an off-white. Flowers have white edges and clusters of white stamens, making the foliage even more striking.

Snow-on-the-mountain grows to about 2 feet high in a somewhat rangy but interesting pattern. It is often included in old-fashioned gardens and is a nice addition to rock or boulder beds. Use in masses or as a border among shrubs. In flower arrangements, prepare cut stems by searing ends with a flame or dip them in boiling water. Be aware the latex that can ooze from cut stems may irritate your skin. Handle with care, being particularly cautious about your eyes or cuts on your hands.

*E. antisyphilitica*, candelilla, has a vertical growth habit, with slender, pale green, leafless stems to 2 feet high or higher. Excellent as a container or accent plant. Plants are cold-tender. Native to Texas.

*E. heterophylla*, Mexican fire plant or wild poinsettia, grows 1 to 2 feet high. The colorful leaves are blotched in bright red and white, similar in appearance to miniature Christmas poinsettias. Flowers are actually showy red *bracts*, modified leaves, and appear from summer into fall. Plants are also tender to frost. Locate in a shaded, protected spot, such as a mini-oasis garden.

**Planting & Care**—These are summer annuals. Sow seed in place 1/16 inch deep after danger of frost has passed. Thin seedlings 6 to 10 inches apart to allow for mature growth. Plants tolerate poor soils. They accept low water after they are established but perform best with additional water during the heat of summer.

## Eustoma grandiflorum — Texas Bluebell, Prairie Gentian

(Also known as *Lisianthus russellianus*.)

The tapered, tuliplike flowers of Texas bluebell are deep purple and bloom mid- to late summer. In recent years, many new forms have been developed in Japan with flower colors in purple, blue, pink and white. Gray-green stems and leaves to 1-1/2 feet support the 2- to 3-inch flowers. For the most profuse blooms, cut flowers frequently and bring them indoors for long-lasting bouquets.

Although classified as an annual or biennial, Texas bluebell can be grown as a short-term perennial. It is an attractive and unusual plant for close-up viewing; plant in pots, boxes and flower borders. Combine with summer-blooming flowers such as *Vinca rosea*, periwinkle, or *Coreopsis* for striking combinations. It is a plant that thrives in hot-summer regions.

**Planting & Care**—Sowing seed can be difficult and time-consuming because seed is small to the point of being dustlike. Sow on soil surface because light is required for germination. Keep soil moist after sowing seed. Seeds germinate in 30 to 90 days. A faster, easier method is to buy established plants from the nursery. Full sun is necessary to develop strong, vigorous growth and consistent flowers. Soil should be loam or sand and well draining but plants will grow in clay soil. Space 18 inches apart to allow for maximum spread. Cut back stems after planting to stimulate more flowering wood, or plants become leggy.

# Gaillardia     Indian Blanket, Blanketflower, Firewheel

*Gaillardia* species are easy-to-grow, dry-climate wildflowers that blend well with low-water subshrubs, ornamental grasses and perennials such as *Coreopsis, Salvia, Rudbeckia* and *Zinnia grandiflora*.

*G. aristata*, blanketflower, is a hardy, richly colored and productive perennial that thrives in sun and heat. It grows 1-1/2 to 2 feet high with 3- to 4-inch, daisylike flowers in shades of red with yellow-tipped petals. The center cushion of the flower is a darker red. Flowers are abundant over a long period during summer and into early fall.

*G. x grandiflora* was developed from crosses of *G. aristata* and *G. pulchella*. Superior selections include 'Golden Goblin' and 'Tangerine'. Plant size and flowering season are similar to *G. aristata* and *G. pulchella*.

*G. pulchella*, firewheel, Indian blanket, is a companion annual to *G. aristata*. It has soft hairy leaves and whiplike stems 2 feet long tipped with 2-inch flowers. Flowers come in shades of red, yellow and gold; the flowering season extends from early summer until frost. Most effective when used in small clusters and in combination with gray-leaved plants. It is often included in western wildflower mixes; its aggressive growth habit allows it to compete well with grasses. Plants are easy to start from seed and care for, useful in meadows, disturbed areas, natural garden plantings and borders.

**Planting & Care**—Plant the fluffy seeds in spring in a sunny spot, covering with 1/8 inch of soil. Ideal soil temperature is 70F to 75F. Does best in light, sterile and well-draining soils. Avoid moist, low-lying locations. Flowers develop in 3 to 4 months depending on temperatures. As with most wildflowers, do not fertilize or you'll encourage foliage growth and have fewer flowers. After establishing seedlings, provide spaced irrigations. Seeds germinate readily in 2 to 5 weeks with warm weather. Space seedlings 1-1/2 to 2 feet apart. Reseeds easily.

Native to prairies of Texas, Nebraska, Colorado and Arizona

Perennial and annual forms; bloom from late spring to fall

Grows 1-1/2 to 2 feet high, spreads 1-1/2 to 2 feet wide

Provide with sand, loam, clay, acid or calcareous soils

Low water use

Plant in full sun; accepts part shade

Seeding rates: 10 grams per 100 sq. ft.; 3 ounces per 500 sq. ft.; 10 pounds per acre

*Gaillardia pulchella*

# Gazania splendens     Gazania

This valuable, colorful ground cover was introduced from South Africa. It is often used as a summer annual in colder climates or as a perennial in temperate regions. It is well adapted to dry-climate regions of the West.

Plants grow in clumps 6 to 12 inches high with leaves that are shiny green on top and silvery white beneath. They bloom continually, producing clusters of daisy flowers 3 to 4 inches across. Flowers come in rich shades of yellow, orange, red and maroon.

Tuck into sunny, small-area gardens, rock gardens and flower borders and as filler or in the foreground between newly planted shrubs. Many other species are available in clumping or trailing forms. 'Red Shades' has become a favorite ground cover for erosion control on slopes or as a lawn substitute in mild, dry-climate regions.

**Planting & Care**—Sow seed 1 inch deep or plant from containers in fall in mild-climate regions. In colder areas plant in spring after danger of frost has passed. Does best in full sun. To plant areas of an acre or more, seed is often applied by *hydromulching*. See page 118. For small areas, apply seed by hand. A regular watering schedule is necessary until young leaves appear. Provide well-spaced irrigations. Inspect top layer of soil to 6-inch depth to see if moisture is needed. Overwatering can cause fungus problems. Performs best in well-draining soils, including sand, loam and decomposed granite. Attention to weed control is important. To renew tired, straggly plants, trim top growth to 3 to 4 inches. Plants can be transplanted. Cut back foliage, dig out and set shovel-size rootball in new location and water thoroughly.

Native to South Africa

Annual or perennial; blooms spring through summer and intermittently all year

Grows 6 to 12 inches high, spreads to 18 inches wide

Accepts any well-draining soil

Low water use

Plant in full sun

Seeding rates: .16 grams per 100 sq. ft.; 5 ounces per 500 sq. ft.; 12 pounds per acre

*Gazania splendens*

*Eustoma grandiflorum,* Texas bluebell, produces tapered, tuliplike flowers from mid- to late summer. Although classified as an annual or biennial, it can be grown as a short-term perennial.

*Gaillardia aristata,* blanketflower, is a hardy, richly colored and productive perennial that thrives in sun and heat. It grows 1-1/2 to 2 feet high with 3- to 4-inch, daisylike flowers in shades of red with yellow-tipped petals. Flowers are abundant over a long period during summer and into early fall.

*Gazania splendens,* gazania, is a South African native often used as a summer annual in colder climates or as a perennial in temperate regions. It is well adapted to dry-climate regions of the West. *Gazania* species make excellent flowering ground covers (below).

*Gilia*
*capitata*

*Gypsophilia*
*paniculata*

## Gilia — Blue Thimble Flower, Globe Gilia

*Gilia capitata* has unique blue flowers that grow in clusters like so many small pincushions. Bloom period is from summer to fall. Tall 2-foot-high stems have 4-inch, finely dissected leaves that create an airy feeling. Plants are quite adaptable, growing well in full sun, partial shade or even full shade. Once established, they require little water. Although native to California, their range is from Alaska and British Columbia east to Idaho.

*G. aggregata*, scarlet gilia (also known as *Ipomopsis aggregata*), is similar with tubular, trumpet-shaped, deep red flowers with star-shaped openings. Unlike *G. capitata*, it flowers from early to late summer. Plants grow from 2 to 2-1/2 feet high.
*G. leptantha*, blue gilia, flowers in spring to midsummer. Best in full sun to partial shade in higher elevations.
*G. tricolor*, bird's-eyes gilia, is a summer bloomer—from June to September. Flower colors range from pale to deep blue-violet. It is distinguished by five pairs of purple spots at the base of each flower petal. Plants grow 10 to 20 inches high.

Use *Gilia* species for color in mass plantings, mixtures and borders. Create striking color combinations with golden California poppy, yellow and white tidy tips, yellow blazing star and red scarlet flax.

**Planting & Care**—Sow seeds in early spring on the surface of well-prepared, well-draining, organic-rich soil. Tamp or roll seed into soil to make good contact. Seedlings will not accept transplanting. Thin to 1 to 1-1/2 feet apart to allow space for growth.

## Gypsophila — Baby's-Breath

Known for its light, airy appearance, *Gypsophila elegans*, baby's-breath, is commonly used by florists in arrangements and by gardeners in flower borders. Growth is open, featuring leaves 3 inches long and single 1/2-inch flowers. Plants are annuals so are short-lived.

*G. paniculata* is a similar perennial form. It is more heavily branched and grows to 3 feet high with slender leaves to 1 inch long. White flowers only 1/16 inch in diameter develop as abundant sprays from midsummer to early fall.

The refined foliage of both annual and perennial forms combined with the small flowers creates a pleasing texture. Plants blend well with other perennials in a mixed border to create an airy, wispy effect. Use in the background of flower beds or as cut or dried flowers. To dry flowers, cut branches and hang in a protected, shaded, well-ventilated location.

**Planting & Care**—Sow seed 1/16 deep in the spring after frost has passed. Seedlings will emerge in 10 to 20 days. For continuous summer bloom, sow seed every month or so to provide an extended flowering season. *G. elegans* will flower the first season. *G. paniculata* requires two seasons before blooming. Plant in place in full sun to partial shade. Space plants widely to allow for spread of 3 to 4 feet. Plants do not transplant easily. Provide with well-draining soil that is not too acid. Once established, plants can become invasive; thin to control.

## Helianthus                                    Sunflower

Sunflowers are one of the most robust flowering annuals you can grow. You might want to give them a try for the pleasure they provide due to their sheer size and for the memories of grandma's garden or a child's first garden.

Reaching 8 to 10 or more feet high with large, coarse, heart-shaped leaves, *Helianthus annuus*, common sunflower, is usually best located at the outer reaches of the landscape, placed against fences or walls. The widely spaced branches support 8- to 10-inch yellow flowers. The cushiony center of the flowers develops into the edible sunflower seeds. The raw seeds are especially enjoyed by birds. Several dwarf introductions are available: 'Autumn Beauty' grows to 3 feet high. 'Teddy Bear' reaches just 2 feet high. Flowers come in crimson, lemon, bronze and mahogany colors.

*H. tuberosus*, Jerusalem artichoke, produces a multitude of yellow flowers to 3-1/2 inches across.

Mature plants can reach 6 to 8 feet high. Large, oval leaves provide a lush foliage effect against walls or fences. As a bonus, the potatolike tubers of Jerusalem artichoke are edible. Harvest tubers in fall.

**Planting & Care**—Sow seeds of sunflower in place 1/2 inch deep during spring in a sunny location. Plant Jerusalem artichoke tubers as you would potatoes. Nutrient-rich soil and regular amounts of deep water early on produce better growth and seedhead production. Avoid crowding plants because roots can be competitive. Space at least 2 to 3 feet apart. Also avoid planting where low roof overhangs or other overhead obstructions could impede growth. Harvest seeds of sunflowers for eating in late fall. Allow plants to dry and then remove stalks.

*Helianthus annuus*

## Hesperis matronalis                        Dame's Rocket

Dame's rocket produces charming, large, phloxlike flower spikes of lilac, mauve, purple and white during late spring into summer. Flowers up to 1 inch across release a delightful fragrance in the evening hours. This multibranched perennial or biennial grows 2 to 3 feet high with lance-shaped to oval leaves 4 inches long.

Dame's rocket has a long history of being cultivated in old gardens and is now seen along roadsides in the East, in regions east of the Rockies to the Atlantic in the South and throughout the West. It is at its best as a background plant in flower borders or in seed mixes that include plants of similar height. Consider placing it near outdoor living areas where its fragrance can be enjoyed. The many spreading branches require about 2 feet of space for adequate spread.

**Planting & Care**—Sow seed 1/16 inch deep in spring. Best in a sunny or partially shaded location. Add organic matter to the soil before planting to

enrich soil and to provide good drainage. Keep soil moist but not soggy. Seed may have to be sown each year to renew planting because plants are short-lived. When temperatures reach the 70F to 75F range, germination takes about 10 to 14 days. Clean up old branching stems in fall to encourage new growth.

Seed of dame's rocket may be hard to find, but the unique fragrance of its flowers make it worth the search.

*Hesperis matronalis*

Right: *Ipomopsis rubra,* Texas plume, is an unusual perennial or biennial that grows 2 to 5 feet high with narrow, cypresslike leaves. Plant stems support tubular, brilliant red flowers that bloom profusely from May into September.

Far right: *Gypsophila elegans,* baby's-breath, is commonly used by florists in arrangements and by gardeners in flower borders. Growth is open, featuring leaves 3 inches long and single 1/2-inch flowers.

*Gilia tricolor,* bird's-eyes gilia, is a summer bloomer—from June to September. Flower colors range from pale to deep blue-violet. It is distinguished by five pairs of purple spots at the base of each flower petal.

Hesperis matronalis, dame's rocket, is a multibranched perennial or biennial that grows 2 to 3 feet high. Place it near outdoor living areas where its fragrance can be enjoyed.

Below left: Helianthus annuus, common sunflower, acts as a border along this walkway. The widely spaced branches support the large yellow flowers.

Below: Lavatera trimestris, rose mallow, produces large, 4-inch, satiny pink flowers. It is an effective plant when used as a tall background or temporary hedge in wide flower borders or among large shrubs.

Perennial or biennial; blooms
late spring through summer

Grows 2 to 5 feet high,
spreads to 2 feet wide

Provide with well-draining,
sandy, loam or gravelly soil

Moderate to high water use

Plant in full sun, partial shade
or tree-dappled shade

Seeding rates: 8 grams per 100
sq. ft.; 2 ounces per 500 sq. ft.;
6 pounds per acre

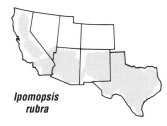

**Ipomopsis
rubra**

---

Native to northern California

Annual; blooms spring
into summer

Grows 6 inches to 2 feet high,
spreads 1-1/2 to 2 feet wide

Accepts most any soil,
even salty soils

Moderate water use

Plant in full sun

Seeding rates: 5 grams per 100
sq. ft.; 1 ounce per 500 sq. ft.;
4 pounds per acre

**Lasthenia
glabrata**

## Ipomopsis — Texas Plume, Red Gilia

*Ipomopsis rubra*, Texas plume (also known as standing cypress), is an unusual perennial or biennial that grows 2 to 5 feet high with narrow, cypresslike leaves. Plant stems support tubular, brilliant red flowers that bloom profusely from May into September. In garden areas, plant in clusters against walls and between shrubs as a filler. It is also a good plant for a wildlife garden, attracting hummingbirds and butterflies. Native to the southeastern U.S., Texas plume is found naturally along river banks from North Carolina to central Florida and west to Texas, Oklahoma and the Southwest.

*I. aggregata* is native to California and is well adapted to dry-climate areas of the Southwest. Flowers are red marked with yellow, and bloom summer to fall. Plants produce tall, single stems 1 to 2-1/2 feet high, making them ideal to mass in clusters as an accent.

**Planting & Care**—Plant nursery-grown seedlings in fall or sow seed in place in spring, planting 1/16 inch deep. Seeds will germinate in about two to three weeks. Be aware plants may not bloom until the second spring. Plants started from seed in winter indoors and set out the following spring after frost will produce flowers the first season. Plants do not transplant well when mature due to deep taproots. Avoid overcrowding—thin seedlings to 2 feet apart to allow for mature spread. Full sun or partial shade is acceptable in most regions. Performs best in light, well-draining soils. To prevent floppy growth, cut flower stems back by one-third in late spring for stronger regrowth.

## Lasthenia glabrata — Goldfields

Goldfields is an annual wildflower native to northern California. It is adapted to most regions in the West, and is included in seed mixes or among perennial flowerbeds. In its native habitat, large masses of goldfields appear as a carpet of gold. Like many wildflowers, they are most likely to flourish when winter and early spring rains are plentiful.

Plants grow 6 to 24 inches high with a multitude of glistening, rich, yellow blooms that look like so many miniature sunflowers. Glossy green leaves are long and slender and create an attractive, bushy background for the prolific, 1-inch flowers. The flowering season lasts from spring into summer. Goldfields is excellent when grown in a container for quick spring color.

*L. chrysostoma*, dwarf goldfields, has the same characteristics as *L. glabrata* but is more compact. It can be found from southern Oregon to southern Arizona at elevations below 3,000 feet.

For spectacular displays in small area gardens, blend either species with *Orthocarpus purpurascens,* owl's clover, or *Linum grandiflorum* 'Rubrum'.

**Planting & Care**—Sow seed in spring in colder areas for quick growth and coverage. Sow seed in fall in mild-climate regions. Sow seed on surface of prepared soil and rake in gently. Keep moist until seedlings germinate, then gradually decrease waterings. Plants have a tolerance for salty soils.

# Lathyrus

**Everlasting Pea, Sweet Pea**

*Lathyrus latifolius,* everlasting pea, is adapted to all climate zones. It grows vigorously as a perennial vine 8 to 10 feet long on a trellis or other support. It can also be grown on slopes and as a ground cover. The flowering season is long, extending from early summer to fall. Once established, plants require minimum attention.

The predominant flower color is reddish purple, but white and rose are often available. Flowers go to seed in profusion and when cut frequently will prolong the bloom period. Plants naturalize readily and should be spaced 3 to 4 feet apart to allow for fast, aggressive growth.

*L. odoratus,* sweet pea, is grown as an annual and is available in separate colors and mixtures as well as bush or vine form.

Provide supports for the 6- to 8-foot-high vines. Bush forms grow to 1-1/2 to 3 feet high. Flowers have a delightful clean and sweet fragrance and are excellent for early spring or summer color in the garden or bouquets indoors. Cut flowers frequently to induce new flowers. 'Bijou', 'Cupid' and 'Little Sweethearts' are superior selections, ideal in patio or courtyard containers for close-up enjoyment. *L. splendens,* pride-of-California, is a striking California native, as its name would indicate. Large, red-purple flowers are absolute show-stoppers, blooming spring to early summer.

**Planting & Care**—Soak seed in water for no more than 24 hours to hasten germination. Treat seed with recommended fungicide to prevent damping-off disease. Sow seed outdoors in a narrow furrow 1-1/2 inches deep. Seedlings emerge in two weeks. After they reach 4 to 6 inches high, pinch off tips to create more branches. Place protective netting over seedlings to keep hungry birds away. Regular moisture as well as a location in full sun are important to establish plants. Cut back plants in late fall for new growth in the spring.

Native to Europe

Perennial; blooms early summer to fall

Grows 6 to 8 feet long as a vine

Provide with well-draining soil improved with organic amendments and balanced fertilizer

Moderate water use when planted in well-prepared soil

Plant in full sun or afternoon shade

Seeding rates: 1 ounce per 50 linear ft.; 8 ounces per 500 sq. ft.

*Lathyrus latifolius*

# Lavatera trimestris

**Rose Mallow**

Rose mallow is an annual that grows rapidly to become a large, shrublike plant to 6 feet high. It is excellent in providing a quick fix for a brand-new home landscape. Plants are often mistaken for hibiscus. Maplelike leaves are 2 inches long and supported by numerous branches. Large, 4-inch, satiny pink flowers bloom through summer and into fall.

This is an effective plant when used as a tall background or temporary hedge in wide flower borders, among large shrubs or along fences and walls. Low-growing varieties in rose-pink, white and bright pink are available. Recommended cultivars include 'Loveliness', deep rose flowers to 4 feet high; 'Mont Blanc' with white flowers and 'Mont Rose' with rose-pink flowers. Both grow to 2 feet high.

Range includes the midwestern and southeastern U.S. Rose mallow is well adapted to the California coast, inland valleys, San Joaquin Valley and low- and middle-elevation deserts.

**Planting & Care**—Plant seeds in spring after danger of frost has passed. Sow 1/8 inch deep in groups of three to five. After seeds germinate in 15 to 30 days, thin to a single, sturdy seedling. Space out groups of seeds to allow for mature spread of 3 to 4 feet. Growth is rapid and vigorous when plants are given regular water. As flowers pass their prime, trim them off to prevent seeds from forming; this will promote more flowers. In windy areas, water deeply to encourage deep roots that anchor plants. Accepts heavy or rich soils; tolerates low pH soils.

Native to the Mediterranean

Annual; blooms summer into fall

Grows 3 to 6 feet high, spreads 3 to 4 feet wide

Provide with almost any soil; accepts soils with low pH

Moderate to high water use

Plant in sunny locations

Seeding rates: 1 ounce per 100 sq. ft.; 4 ounces per 500 sq. ft.; 20 pounds per acre

*Lavatera trimestris*

*Layia platyglossa compestris*

*Liatris spicata*

## Layia platyglossa compestris     Tidy-Tips

This is a low-growing annual from 8 to 18 inches high, producing a carpet of bright yellow flowers tipped with a white fringe. Flowers bloom prolifically for several months beginning in early spring. Seeds can also be sown in late spring in cold-winter regions, providing flowers later in the season—to June and beyond. Natural range is from Baja California along coastal California to Napa and Mendocino counties. Plants grow on open grassy hillsides, valley floors and disturbed land.

*L. glandulosa* is a related species, native to Arizona. It produces pure white flowers.

Tidy-tips is a colorful and attractive plant when viewed from above, which makes it excellent for low containers and window boxes. Flowers literally cover the small, lance-shaped leaves. It is included in many seed mixes for its early flowers. Sow seed according to rates supplied here to create a thick carpet of color.

**Planting & Care**—In cold-winter regions sow seed in early spring as it begins to warm. Sow seed in the fall months in mild-winter climates. Sow 1/16 inch deep. Seeds germinate rapidly in a week or two and flowering begins in 6 to 8 weeks. Tidy-tips prefers full sun and accepts either heavy loam or light sandy soil. It also tolerates a wide soil pH range. Water requirements are low after plants have developed three to five leaves. Water deeply every week to help encourage a deep root system. Naturalizes after one or two seasons.

## Liatris     Gay-Feather

*Liatris* species are wonderful low-maintenance perennials that provide exclamation points of rose-pink, magenta or white. The 6- to 9-inch spikes bloom from late summer into late fall. Color during this period is most appreciated, since this is the time most flowering perennials begin to go into dormancy. The stiff stems have thin grassy leaves below the flower clusters, which open from the top downward. The flower stems grow 2 to 5 feet high and are long lasting as cut flowers in arrangements. A mature plant may produce a dozen or more flowering wands.

Include in the perennial border or in a wildflower or natural garden. Once established, this North American native tolerates dry conditions. *Liatris* also attracts bees and butterflies.

*L. punctata*, spotted gay feather, produces dense purple flower spikes to 2 feet high. Blooms late summer and fall.

*L. scariosa alba* 'White Spire' grows to 3 feet, has flowers of pure white. *L. spicata* 'Kobold' is a dwarf, growing to about 1-1/2 feet, with flowers of deep rose-pink. It is excellent used in the rock garden.

**Planting & Care**—Divide and plant in spring or fall, or sow seeds 1/16 inch deep indoors in pots in early fall for spring planting. Slow to grow from seed; stratification may hasten germination. Plants are becoming more readily available in containers at nurseries. Space plants 12 to 18 inches apart (12 inches apart if planting in groups or masses). Provide with well-draining soil in full sun; filtered shade in hot climates is desirable. Moderate moisture before and during flowering produces better and longer-lasting blooms. Plants go dormant in the winter but recover by spring. They are long lasting and become a reliable part of the garden.

*Layia platyglossa compestris,* tidy-tips, is favored for its prolific flowers and long bloom period that begins in early spring. It is a colorful and attractive plant when viewed from above.

Below left: *Lasthenia glabrata,* goldfields, is an annual wildflower native to northern California. It is adapted to most regions in the West.

Below: *Lathyrus odoratus,* sweet pea, is grown as an annual. It is available in separate colors and mixtures as well as bush or vine forms. Flowers have a delightful sweet fragrance.

**Native to California**

—

Annual; blooms spring
into summer

—

Grows 3 to 14 inches high,
spreads 6 to 12 inches wide

—

Provide with well-draining
sandy or loam soil

—

Moderate water use extends
flowering season;
low water use otherwise

—

Plant in full sun or partial shade

—

Seeding rates: 5 grams per 100
sq. ft.; 1 ounce per 500 sq. ft.;
4 pounds per acre

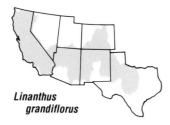

Linanthus
grandiflorus

**Native to Morocco**

—

Perennial and annual; bloom
from spring to summer

—

Grows 8 inches to 2 feet high,
spreads 1 foot wide

—

Provide with light,
well-draining soil

—

Low water use

—

Plant in sun or partial shade

—

Seeding rates: 10 grams per 100
sq. ft.; 3 ounces per 500 sq. ft.;
1 pound per acre

Linaria
maroccana

## Linanthus grandiflorus — Mountain Phlox

*Linanthus grandiflorus* is a California native widely adapted to the western United States. Mountain phlox produces dense clusters of delicate white flowers tinged with a soft lilac blush. Colors can vary greatly from pink and pale lavender to white. Flowers are surrounded by refined leaves on slender upright stems. Growth can be rampant to 1 to 1-1/2 feet high, with a bloom period that extends from spring into summer.

Mountain phlox has many uses. Include it in flower borders or on slopes or plant in masses in open, woodland settings. Combine with *Linum grandiflorum* 'Rubrum' for an exciting show of color.

*L. aureus*, desert gold, is a ground-hugging plant, growing 4 to 6 inches high. Flowers are bright yellow and bloom during spring and into summer. Well adapted to desert areas in the Southwest, doing best in sandy soils.

**Planting & Care**—Sow seed in place in fall or early spring. Plant 1/4 to 1/2 inch deep. Does best in well-draining sandy or loam soil. Full sun is important for best growth. Seedlings emerge in just a few weeks and flowers bloom in 8 to 12 weeks. Thin plants so they are spaced about 1 foot apart to allow for natural spread. Once established, water requirements are low. In low-rainfall regions, increase watering during dry periods to keep flowers coming.

## Linaria — Baby Snapdragon, Spurred Snapdragon, Toadflax

*Linaria maroccana*, spurred snapdragon, is a fast-growing annual adapted to a wide range of western climates. The delicate flowers bloom on top of tall, narrow stems in colors that range from red, pink and gold to violet and purple. Plants grow from 1 to 2 feet high and look best when planted as a mass display. The stems are rather sturdy, which allows plants to compete well with grasses and in wildflower mixes.

*L. reticulata* 'Aureo-purpurea', purple-net toadflax, grows 8 to 12 inches high and blooms earlier in the spring than *L. maroccana*. Flowers come in clusters of striking purple and gold on top of light green leaves. Use in mass plantings or wildflower mixes. Well adapted to difficult growing conditions, such as those found at the perimeter of the landscape. In garden beds, locate in the background behind low-growing wildflowers such as phlox, scarlet flax and scarlet sage. Prefers light shade.

**Planting & Care**—Sow seed where you want plants to grow in spring in cold-winter areas. Sow in fall in mild-winter regions. Cast seed on soil surface, tamping with your feet to make good contact. Prefers light, sterile soils. Grows well in sun or partial shade. Water requirement is low after plants are established. Plants are easy to grow and reseed readily.

# Linum

### Scarlet Flax, Wild Blue Flax

*Linum grandiflorum* 'Rubrum', scarlet flax, is a star performer in the world of western wildflowers and produces some of the most colorful displays. Its strongly vertical flowering stems are striking in solid masses or in mixtures. The intense red flowers, 1 to 1-1/2 inches wide, are profuse and stand out from the lush, narrow, grayish green leaves. Each individual flower lasts only one day, but the large quantity of flowers produce a show of color from spring until summer.

Plants are well adapted to North America especially in the high heat regions of low- and middle-elevation deserts. The colorful flowers are included in many seed mixes. Competes well with grasses. Outstanding when planted in combination with gray-foliaged plants such as brittle bush, rosemary and lavender, or with the golden yellow California poppy.

*L. perenne lewisii*, wild blue flax, is a perennial that produces a bouquet of sky blue during summer and into fall.

Plants grow to 2 feet high and blend well with other wildflowers because of their narrow leaves, which do not crowd surrounding plants. Growth is vase-shaped with an airy look. A useful color plant in cool climates or for winter color in mild-climate areas. Native to California.

*L. narbonense* is a similar species with wiry stems and clusters of 1-3/4-inch, white-eyed, azure-blue flowers.

**Planting & Care**—In mild-winter climates, sow seed in place in the fall. In cold-winter climates, sow seed in spring after danger of frost has passed. Cover seed with 1/16 inch of soil. With 70F temperatures, seeds germinate in 20 to 25 days, with flowers appearing in 10 to 12 weeks. Best in full sun in well-draining soil. Thin seedlings after they reach 2 to 3 inches high to 4 to 6 inches apart. Plants will develop more flowering stems. Overly moist, soggy soils produce weak plants. Water requirement is low to moderate after plants are established.

L. grandiflorum native to North Africa;
L. lewisii native to California

---

Annual and perennial; blooms spring to midsummer

---

Grows 1 to 2 feet high, spreads 6 to 9 inches wide

---

Provide with well-draining soil improved with organic matter

---

Low water use

---

Plant in full sun

---

Seeding rates: 12 grams per 100 sq. ft.; 4 ounces per 500 sq. ft.; 8 pounds per acre

**Linum grandiflorum 'Rubrum'**

# Lobelia cardinalis

### Cardinal Flower

The flame red spikes of cardinal flower appear on upright stems 1 to 6 feet high, providing dramatic stature and color for the summer season. Stems are covered with 2- to 3-inch sawtooth leaves. The tubular flowers look like honeysuckle blooms and are loved by hummingbirds. Cardinal flower is native to the eastern U.S. When planted in shady, moist locations it is widely adapted throughout the West.

*L. cardinalis var. splendens* inhabits moist and boggy locations in the San Gabriel Mountains and San Bernardino Mountains south to San Diego County, east to Texas and into Mexico. It is one of the few perennial wildflowers that do well in shady or sunny locations, provided it has adequate moisture. Plants grow 1-1/2 to 2-1/2 feet high with individual flowers to 1-1/2 inches long.

*L. dunnii var. serrata*, blue lobelia, is a choice, low-growing plant to 10 inches. Pale blue flowers contrast against dark green leaves. Excellent for moist, shady locations.

Use *Lobelia* species in combination with similar-sized plants; they tend to overshadow plants of smaller stature. Blend into the back of wide flower borders and in masses along walls.

**Planting & Care**—Sowing seed in the fall usually works best. Sow on soil surface and tamp to make good contact. Allow about two months after seeding for plants to develop to transplant size. Container-grown seedlings accept transplanting. Locate in sun or in the partial shade of large, open canopy trees that have similar moisture needs. Plants require a rich soil and regular moisture. Try them along drainage swales or dry creek beds. Using a mulch around plant roots also increases moisture retention. Allow about 2 feet of space between plants for adequate spread. Plants reseed freely. Well-established plants can be divided in early spring.

Native to eastern U.S. and the U.S. southwest in moist, high-elevation locations

---

Tender perennial; blooms spring and summer

---

Grows 1 to 6 feet high, spreads 1 to 2 feet wide

---

Provide with well-draining soil

---

Moderate to high water use

---

Full sun to partial shade

---

Seeding rates: 3 grams per 100 sq. ft.; .5 ounces per 500 sq. ft.; 2 pounds per acre

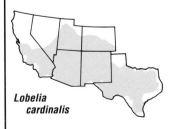

**Lobelia cardinalis**

Above: *Lobularia maritima*, sweet alyssum, is a sure-blooming, low-growing annual with a prolific, textured flowering habit. It is often used to complement more brightly colored flowers, such as these yellow pansies.

Above right: *Linaria reticulata* 'Aureo-purpurea', purple-net toadflax, is frequently included in mass plantings or wildflower mixes. It is adapted to difficult growing conditions, such as those common to the landscape perimeter.

Right: *Lupinus succulentus*, arroyo lupine or succulent lupine, is one of the easiest lupines to grow. It reaches 2 to 4 feet high, producing attractive flowers in shades of blue or pink.

## Lobularia maritima — Sweet Alyssum

Sweet alyssum is a sure-blooming, low-growing annual with a prolific, textured flowering habit. It has many uses and can be included in garden borders, rock gardens and containers and on slopes for rapid revegetation. It also works well as a colorful, fast-growing, temporary ground cover until permanent landscape plants have a chance to mature. Use as a solid color in a pattern planting or blend several varieties for a colorful mosaic of flowers.

The small flower clusters of sweet alyssum have a delightful, honeylike fragrance. Flowers bloom in late winter and spring in mild climates and desert areas, and bloom spring, summer and fall in cooler areas.

The white form 'Carpet of Snow' reseeds vigorously and can even become a pesky weed. However, roots are rather shallow, so it's easy to pull up and discard unwanted plants. Varieties available include 'Rosie O'Day', deep rose, and purple 'Royal Carpet'. 'Snow Crystals' has large, dazzling white flowers and persists well into hot weather. All self-sow, but seedlings gradually seem to revert to lighter, less dramatic colors and more rangy growth.

**Planting & Care**—Sow seed in sunny areas in fall in mild climates and desert areas; sow in spring in cold areas. Locate in a sunny spot; too much shade causes growth to be spindly. Sow seeds on soil surface and tamp to make good contact. Seeds germinate in about one week and flowers bloom within one or two months with warm weather. Thin seedlings 6 to 8 inches apart to allow for spread. After plants have bloomed for a few months, trim back at least one-third to induce a new surge of growth and flowers. Prefers moderate moisture, but tolerates low water use, heat, wind and salt air.

Native to the shores of the Mediterranean Sea

Annual; blooms all year in mild-winter climates; spring to fall in cold regions

Grows to 1 foot high, spreads 1 to 1-1/2 feet wide

Provide with most any soil

Low to moderate water use

Plant in full sun

Seeding rates: 8 grams per 100 sq. ft.; 2 ounces per 500 sq. ft.; 6 pounds per acre

*Lobularia maritima*

## Lupinus — Texas Bluebonnet, Lupine

*Lupinus texensis*, Texas bluebonnet, is known for its sweeping displays of upright, rich blue flowers. Tips of flower petals are white, then as flowers age they take on tones of reddish purple. This colorful bloom cycle occurs from March into May in Texas. In mild-climate regions, warmer weather causes the flowers to bloom earlier. Texas bluebonnet is a most colorful, low-growing addition to mixes or use as a mass planting. Plants grow 1 to 2 feet high and work well in narrow, sunny flower beds among shrub borders and in rock gardens. As a bonus, they have a most pleasant fragrance. See photo, page 17.

*L. densiflorus aureus*, golden lupine, an annual native to California, is well known and widely distributed in the West. The pealike golden flowers stand erect above the leaves. Mature height is 1-1/2 to 2 feet with a similar spread. *L. nanus*, blue and white lupine, annual lupine, is a California native. Branches form at the base with stems that reach 8 to 24 inches high. Flowers are predominantly blue but are sometimes white or pink.

*L. succulentus*, arroyo lupine (also called succulent lupine), is often considered the easiest lupine to grow. It reaches 2 to 4 feet high, producing attractive flowers in shades of blue or pink. It is found in the wild in ravines and along hillsides and roadsides throughout California.

**Planting & Care**—Soak seed in hot (180F to 200F) water for no more than 24 hours prior to seeding to improve germination, or scratch the hard seed coat. With this treatment, germination should occur in 2 to 8 weeks after temperatures reach the 60F range. Sow seed in the fall where plants are to be located, covering with 1/8 inch of soil. Keep the soil moist until seedlings sprout. Thin seedlings 9 to 12 inches apart. Once established, provide deep irrigation about every two weeks if rainfall is lacking. Lupines enjoy deep, well-draining soils but will thrive in poor or sandy soils.

Native to the U.S. Southwest

Annual; blooms early spring to early summer; blooms during summer along coast

Grows 1-1/2 to 4 feet high, spreads 1-1/2 to 2 feet wide

Provide with well-draining sand or loam soil

Low water use

Plant in full sun

Seeding rates: 1 gram per 100 sq. ft.; .25 ounces per 500 sq. ft.; 15 pounds per acre

*Lupinus texensis*

*Lychnis chalcedonica*

## Lychnis chalcedonica                  Maltese-Cross

The flower color of Maltese-cross, also called Jerusalem cross, is one of the most brilliant in the scarlet range. Individual, deeply cut petals form a distinct cross within the flower that is striking in appearance. Flowers form in dense, terminal clusters and bloom profusely in midsummer. The 2- to 4-inch hairy leaves are carried on stout stems that grow to 3 feet high, giving the plant an open appearance. Plants prefer cool coastal climates but can be grown successfully in warmer regions if given afternoon shade and shelter. Use in wide flower beds as a backdrop with white-flowering or gray-foliaged plants.

Selections such as 'Alba', white flowers, and *Lychnis x haageana*, mixed colors, provide options for flower colors that include crimson, orange, rose, salmon, pink with stripes and white. Plant in clusters spaced 3 to 4 feet apart for a dramatic effect.

**Planting & Care**—Sow seeds on the soil surface and keep soil moist.

Prefers well-draining soil. Seedlings emerge in two to three weeks when temperatures are 70F to 80F. Thin while they are small. As plant stems develop, cut back tips of branches to encourage more branching stems. Provide low to moderate moisture after plants are established. Accepts full sun to light shade; plants tend to sprawl in deep shade. Deadhead spent flower stems. Plants reseed readily. Perennial forms can be divided with age.

*Malcolmia maritima*

## Malcolmia maritima        Virginia Stock, Malcolm Stock

For late spring and early summer color, Virginia stock is an excellent choice. This annual grows rapidly and flowers easily. Include it in rock gardens, as a bulb cover and in flower beds placed behind borders of white sweet alyssum or snow-in-summer. It's also effective when planted in containers. For best results, select low-profile pots so you can look down on the branching stems and flowers.

Dwarfish, 8- to 15-inch, single or branching stems support small, vigorous flowers. Flower colors include white, pink, yellow and lilac to magenta. Unlike other stocks, the flower fragrance is light.

**Planting & Care**—Sow seed in place in early spring after frost has passed. Moisten soil to 8 inches deep before planting. Plant seed 1/8 to 1/4 inch deep. Locate in full sun in a moderately rich soil amended with organic matter. Flowers develop in 6 to 10 weeks after seeding. Provide regular water but do not overwater. After the

first bursts of bloom and as plants complete flowering, remove dead flowerheads for a cleaner appearance. Plants do not reseed well and usually must be replanted each season. However, growing Virginia stock is well worth the effort because of the abundance of colorful flowers that are produced.

## Mentzelia lindleyi    Blazing-Star

This is a tall, wide-spreading biennial, growing 1 to 4 feet high and up to 2 feet wide. Its appearance is like that of a dwarf shrub. Clusters of yellow flowers with reddish orange centers and yellow stamens are real eye-catchers and are well suited in the natural border. Plants produce hundreds of stems that create a mounding effect. Bloom period is spring into early summer. Foliage has a rough-textured appearance like that of dandelions; the lower leaves can be as long as 6 to 8 inches. Short barbed hairs are located at the tips of leaves.

Blazing-star is useful in wildflower mixes. It tolerates difficult conditions of poor soil, heat and wind and competes well with weeds due to its tall growth. Plant in masses—alone or combine with bachelor's-button and blue thimble flower—for a colorful scene. Plants are ideal for viewing from a distance because of their height and striking colors. They are also effective in revegetating disturbed areas. If used this way, combine with *Argemone platyceras*, prickly poppy. It is described on page 107.

**Planting & Care**—Sow seed on soil surface in place in fall, winter or spring, raking lightly into soil. Regular moisture is important until flowers develop, then reduce or cease watering. Grows best in full sun. Accepts heavy to light soils, rich or sterile, as long as soil is well draining.

Native to Mt. Hamilton range of the California coast and inland to Fresno County

Biennial; blooms spring into early summer

Grows 1 to 4 feet high, spreads 1-1/2 to 2 feet wide

Provide with light sandy soils; accepts heavy soils

Moderate water use until flowers develop, then no water

Plant in full sun

Seeding rates: 5 grams per 100 sq. ft.; 1 ounce per 500 sq. ft.; 4 pounds per acre

*Mentzelia lindleyi*

## Mimulus cardinalis    Scarlet Monkey Flower

Scarlet monkey flower is known for its long, alternate, light green leaves that are sharply toothed and sticky. Flowers are scarlet to orange, 1-1/2 to 2 inches long on somewhat floppy stems. The flowering season extends from July into October with heat, but moisture needs are constant during warm periods. Plants grow from 2 to 4 feet high and sprawl 2 to 4 feet wide.

This group of plants requires shade to grow properly. Some of the best locations for scarlet monkey flower are in groupings along shaded boulder beds and alongside dry streambeds, particularly beneath canopies of wide-spreading trees. A shaded environment is essential in inland and hot-summer areas. In coastal gardens, monkey flower is more tolerant of direct sun.

**Planting & Care**—Sow seed in the fall or set out container-grown plants in spring. Prefers well-draining soil high in organic matter. After plants bloom early in the season, prune flowering stems to cause the plant to produce more flowering wood. Under the best conditions, flowering may continue most of the year. Increase desirable plants by rooting cuttings in moist sand; transplant when cuttings are well rooted. Older plants also develop underground rootstock that can easily be divided and transplanted. Plants in densely shaded locations eventually become straggly. When this occurs, prune back plants severely after first bloom and a second flush of flowers will follow.

Native to southern Oregon, California, Utah, Nevada and Arizona

Perennial; blooms summer into fall

Grows 2 to 4 feet high, spreads 2 to 3 feet wide

Provide with well-draining soil high in organic matter

Moderate to high water use

Plant in full sun along coast; in partial shade in hot inland areas

Seeding rates: 4 grams per 100 sq. ft.; 1 ounce per 500 sq. ft.

*Mimulus cardinalis*

*Malcolmia maritima,* Virginia stock, is one of the best annual wildflowers for late spring and early summer color. Dwarfish plants produce single or branching stems that support small, vigorous flowers in shades of white, pink, yellow and lilac to magenta.

*Lychnis chalcedonica,* Maltese-cross, produces brilliant scarlet flowers in midsummer. Individual, deeply cut petals form a distinct cross within the flower that is striking in appearance.

Above left: *Mimulus cardinalis,* scarlet monkey flower, is known for its brilliant, scarlet to orange flowers that bloom midsummer into fall.

Above: *Linum grandiflorum* 'Rubrum', red flax, produces one of the brightest reds of any flower. Plants are well adapted to hot, dry conditions.

Left: *Mentzelia lindleyi,* blazing-star, blooms spring to early summer. Plants produce clusters of yellow flowers with reddish orange centers and yellow stamens that are real eye-catchers.

**Mirabilis jalapa**

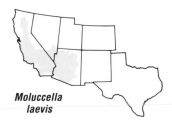

**Moluccella laevis**

# Mirabilis — Giant Four O'Clock, Beauty-of-the-Night

*Mirabilis jalapa*, giant four o'clock, is a summer annual where temperatures drop below 20F, a perennial in milder climates. It is native to tropical South America yet is well adapted to all desert areas. Growth is rapid, almost shrublike to 3 feet high and nearly as wide. It is an ideal plant for the natural garden. Be aware that plants can be invasive, with a huge root system. Large, oval leaves are deep green and clothe the plant, creating a bushy appearance. The shrubby form provides a green backdrop for annuals or perennials that grow from 1-1/2 to 3 feet high. Clusters of fragrant, trumpet-shaped flowers, 1-1/2 to 2 inches long, come in shades of red, pink, yellow or white. Many times flowers have a striped or mottled pattern. The flowers also have a unique habit of opening in midafternoon.

*M. multiflora*, desert four o'clock, is a multibranched perennial that grows to 1 foot high with a spread to 4 feet. It is native to the Four Corners region of Utah, Colorado, Arizona and New Mexico. Flowers of giant four-o'clock are available in shades of pink to magenta. They bloom from mid-summer to early fall.

**Planting & Care**—Cold-stratify seed by storing in a sealed jar in the refrigerator for three months before planting. Sow seed 1/4 inch deep in place. Sow in fall in mild regions; wait until spring after danger of frost has passed in cold regions. Open, sunny locations are ideal. Tolerates heat, wind, air pollution and sandy soil. Deep moisture is important to establish plants. After tubers develop, plants become relatively low-water users. Thin seedlings to allow for 3- to 4-foot spread of mature plants. Thin or prune branches to shape and control growth. As plants of *M. multiflora* mature, the roots develop into tubers similar to dahlia roots. Store over winter in cold-climate areas and plant again in spring. Plants reseed easily or plant tubers during the winter-dormant period.

# Moluccella laevis — Bells-of-Ireland, Shellflower

Bells-of-Ireland is a favorite spring and summer annual, excellent for close-up viewing. Flowers grow on stems and branches 1-1/2 to 2 feet high.

Whorls of six individual apple-green flowers cover the stems from the base to the top. The crispy, upper- and lower-lipped flowers are appealing in flower arrangements and last for a long time. They can even be used as dried flowers. To dry, cut prime flowers, remove leaves and hang in protected, well-ventilated location.

The most dramatic way to use bells-of-Ireland is in clusters in the background of flower beds with 1- to 1-1/2-foot annuals in the foreground. Sunny locations are important for good appearance and growth. East or south exposure along a wall in combination with dark green shrubs creates an ideal background for the interesting flowers. Use in clusters of three for the most striking effect.

**Planting & Care**—Prepare soil so that it is well draining and has a loose, friable texture. In dry-climate regions, plant seed in the fall months. In cold-winter areas, sow in spring after danger of frost has passed. If fall weather remains warm prior to planting seed, refrigerate seed for 10 days prior to sowing. Sow in place or set out plants from containers, available at some nurseries. Shelter plants from extreme winds. Regular soil moisture will keep flowers producing, but do not overwater.

# Monarda

### Bee Balm, Oswego Tea, Horsemint

*M*onarda didyma, bee balm, is a perennial wildflower that produces stunning clusters of tubular, scarlet-red flowers. Many hybrids and selections are also available in rose-red, scarlet and pink. The prolific stalks grow 2 to 3 feet high. Loved by hummingbirds, the flowers bloom for a long period in summer. Fragrant, oval, long, dark green leaves have a strong scent reminiscent of basil blended with mint.

Plants are best adapted to regions with cool summers, such as areas along the coast. They are not long-lived in areas of long, hot summers. In these warm regions, locate where they'll receive some afternoon shade and plant in well-prepared, organic-rich soil that will retain moisture. Place in garden borders as a tall background with low-growing perennials and annuals that have a similar moderate to high water requirement. Natural habitat is along streambeds. The following species are adapted to dry-climate areas.

*M. austromontana* is native to southeast Arizona, New Mexico and northern Mexico. Plants grow to 1-1/2 feet high. The whitish flowers bloom late spring and early summer.

*M. citriodora*, horsemint or lemonmint, is native to Utah, Texas and Arizona. It is more tolerant of heat than bee balm. Plants grow 1-1/2 to 2 feet high, spreading 1 foot wide. Clusters of flower spikes in pink or white reach 6 inches high and bloom from mid-spring to early summer. Flowers have a delightful lemon scent.

**Planting & Care**—Sow seeds in place, singly or in clusters, after danger of frost has passed. Thin seedlings 1 to 1-1/2 feet apart to allow for spread. Avoid watering at night to reduce rust disease, which is prone to attack the foliage. Cut back to a few inches above ground level in late fall after flowering. Divide every three to four years in spring to encourage new basal growth.

**Native to North America**

**Perennial; blooms midspring to summer, depending on species**

**Grows 1-1/2 to 3 feet high with an equal spread**

**Provide with amended, well-draining soil**

**Moderate water use**

**Plant in full sun along coast; provide afternoon shade in hot-summer regions**

**Seeding rates: 20 grams per 100 sq. ft.; 8 ounces per 500 sq. ft.; 16 pounds per acre**

*Monarda didyma*

# Myosotis

### Forget-Me-Not

*M*yosotis sylvatica, forget-me-not, is ideal for partially shaded locations where it is sometimes difficult to get color plants to thrive. Small, clear blue flowers with white eyes bloom generously from early spring until midsummer, loosely covering upper stems and foliage. The soft, simple, hairy leaves grow 1/2 to 2 inches long.

Forget-me-not is most useful as a lush, colorful ground cover among shade-loving shrubs, blending with other plants in the shaded border. It is a persistent grower that reseeds easily. It is usually grown as an annual but can be grown as a biennial in mild-climate regions. Its growth pattern is suited to natural garden designs, particularly beneath a canopy of trees or near a shaded patio.

*M. alpestris* 'Blue Bell' grows as a compact, ball-shaped plant. Bright blue flowers are ideal for edging and as a solid planting. 'Victoria Mixed' also has a compact growth habit, growing to just 6 inches high. Flowers are a uniform mixture of white, blue, rose and pink.

**Planting & Care**—Sow seeds in place in fall in mild-winter areas for color the following spring. In cold-winter areas, sow seed in early spring. Cover lightly with soil, but cover seeds completely because darkness is required for germination. Seedlings generally emerge in two to four weeks at 70F temperatures. Plants are also available at the nursery in containers and can be propagated by cuttings taken in summer. Improve soils by adding organic amendments, and provide regular moisture until plants are established. Plants generally grow vigorously and may need heavy thinning to reduce crowding.

**Native to Eurasia and Europe**

**Annual or biennial; blooms early spring to midsummer**

**Grows 6 to 15 inches high, spreads 15 to 18 inches wide**

**Provide with amended, well-draining soil with pH from acid to neutral**

**High to moderate water use**

**Plant in partial shade**

**Seeding rates: 4 grams per 100 sq. ft.; 1 ounce per 500 sq. ft.**

*Myosotis sylvatica*

*Above: Mirabilis multiflora,* desert four o'clock, is a multibranched plant that grows to 1 feet high with a spread to 4 feet. It is native to the Four Corners region of Utah, Colorado, Arizona and New Mexico.

*Myosotis sylvatica,* forget-me-not, is useful as a lush, colorful ground cover among shade-loving shrubs. It is a persistent grower that reseeds easily.

*Moluccella laevis,* bells-of-Ireland, is a favorite spring and summer annual, excellent for close-up viewing. Use in clusters in the background of flower beds with 1- to 1-1/2-foot annuals in the foreground. A sunny location is important for good appearance and growth.

*Monarda didyma,* bee balm, is a perennial wildflower that produces clusters of tubular, scarlet-red flowers. Plants are best adapted to regions with cool summers, such as areas along the coast.

**Native to Sierra Nevada foothills of western U.S.**

---

**Annual; blooms spring through summer along coast; ceases early summer in warmer regions**

---

**Grows to 6 inches high, spreads 12 to 15 inches wide**

---

**Provide with well-draining soil improved with organic matter**

---

**Moderate water use in cool climates; high other regions**

---

**Plant in partial shade**

---

**Seeding rates: 10 grams per 100 sq. ft.; 5 ounces per 500 sq. ft.; 20 pounds per acre**

*Nemophila menziesii*

**Native to Caucasus, Eurasia**

---

**Perennial; blooms early summer to early fall**

---

**Grows 1 to 2 feet high, spreads 1 to 2 feet wide**

---

**Tolerates most any well-draining soil**

---

**Moderate to high water use depending on summer temperatures**

---

**Plant in full sun**

---

**Seeding rates: 4 grams per 100 sq. ft.; 1 ounce per 500 sq. ft.**

*Nepeta cataria*

# Nemophila                                    Baby-Blue-Eyes

The cup-shaped, sky blue and white-eyed flowers of *Nemophila menziesii*, baby-blue-eyes, are ideally used as a low cover among bulb plantings. Flowers appear from March through May in warm regions. In cool coastal areas flowers bloom from early spring well into summer. Baby-blue-eyes is native to California with a range through the western U.S., including Nevada County to Kern County in the Sierra Nevada foothills. It is not adapted to hot or humid locations. Plants should also be located where they'll be protected from strong winds.

*N. maculata*, five-spot nemophila, is similar in appearance to baby-blue-eyes but has purple lines and a large purple dot on each flower petal. Flowers reach 1 to 2 inches in diameter. It is also native to the Sierra Nevada foothills. Both species are useful in border plantings or when allowed to naturalize in rock gardens and in containers. Unlike many native plants, five-spot nemophila appreciates light applications of fertilizer during the early part of its growing season.

**Planting & Care**—Add organic matter to soil to provide a loose, well-draining seedbed. If used as a bulb cover, plant the same time as bulbs. Sow seeds in place in spring in cold climates; sow in fall in mild-winter areas. Cover seed lightly with soil. Seeds germinate in about 2 weeks or less, flowering in 6 to 8 weeks. Thin to 12 inches apart. Reseeds readily in moist, shady locations. Supply with moderate to high moisture for best growth and appearance.

# Nepeta                                         Catnip, Catmint

The distinct, aromatic foliage of *Nepeta cataria*, catnip, is irresistible to cats, who like to roll around in the leaves. Gardeners are more apt to enjoy the clustered spikes of violet flowers with white spots that appear in early summer. Plants are perennial and grow 1 to 2 feet high with a low branching habit and unique, square-shaped stems with silvery gray leaves. Native to Eurasia.

*N. x faassenii*, catmint (often sold as *N. mussinii*), has a more undulating growth habit, reaching 2 feet high. Lavender-blue flowers are produced in loose spikes in early to midsummer. Leaves are attractive gray-green. Catmint, as its name indicates, is also favored by cats. Allow plenty of space for the spreading growth. Native to the Caucasus.

Either species works well as a ground cover, in rock gardens or in a natural garden, their forms, colors and textures blending well with other low-water-use plants. Use in the foreground to taller flowering shrubs.

**Planting & Care**—Sow seed in place 1/4 inch deep or plant from containers in fall or early spring. Space container-planted plants on 3-foot centers. Locate in full sun in well-drained soil. Provide regular water in warm climate zones and moderate water in more temperate or coastal areas. After flowers have completed their bloom period, trim spent flower tips to encourage additional flush of bloom. Plants reseed. If cats disturb plants, cut back damaged growth to stimulate renewal.

# Oenothera

Primrose

These easy-to-grow annuals and perennials have blossoms that open only during the day or only at night, depending on the species. Flowers are often yellow, sometimes white or pale pink. They have four petals in an open, buttercup shape, with a cluster of fluffy yellow stamens at the center. *Calyxes,* the sepals underneath the petals, are often bright red and showy. *Oenothera* spreads by underground runners and will quickly colonize.

*O. berlandieri,* Mexican evening primrose, flowers from late spring into summer with rose-pink, 1-1/2-inch flowers on stems 10 to 12 inches high. Perennial plants can be invasive and overgrow smaller, less-aggressive plants. Native to Mexico and Texas. *O. caespitosa,* white evening primrose, also known as tufted evening primrose, is native to the U.S. Southwest. It has a unique, rounded growth habit with long, sword-shaped, gray-green leaves. Plants grow in clumps less than 1 foot high and to 3 feet wide. White flowers (turning pink as they age) to 2 to 3 inches across open in the evening hours and close the next morning. Hardy to 5F.

*O. speciosa* is a daytime-flowering plant growing 1 to 2 feet high with coarse brown stems. Flowers are white, changing to pink as they age, and bloom for a long period from spring into summer. Plants become dormant during winter.

*O. stubbei,* Baja evening primrose, has yellow flowers 2-1/2 inches wide that rise 8 inches above the dark green leaves. Well adapted to southwest desert areas. Perennial. Native to Baja California.

**Planting & Care**—Plants are available at nurseries in containers for fall or early spring planting. Or sow seed in fall or spring, covering lightly. Grow in full sun, spacing 1-1/2 feet apart for upright growers, 2 feet apart for spreading forms. Occasionally, worms will infest plantings. Plants usually recover quickly. Divide existing plantings in early spring or take stem cuttings in late summer.

*Oenothera berlandieri*

# Orthocarpus purpurascens

Owl's Clover

Owl's clover is an annual wildflower well suited to perennial or annual flower beds that flower well ahead of the spring color surge. Plants can be parasitic on the roots of grasses and obtain some of their nutrients this way. But they can also be grown alone. Owl's clover is especially attractive tucked into out-of-the-way places in the garden, on slopes and in rock gardens.

When fall rains are plentiful, there's a good chance that by early spring stretches of the western Mojave desert are covered with owl's clover blooms. Plants do best at elevations of 2,000 to 3,000 feet. The native range also extends to southern and western Arizona.

The dense terminal clusters of 1- to 1-1/2 inch cloverlike heads feature vivid colors of rose-pink or purple— the lower lips of flowers are tipped in yellow. Plant stems are erect with each stem full of color. Companion plants include blue-flowering *Phacelia campanularia,* page 91, California bluebells, California poppy, *Eschscholzia californica,* page 59, and *Linum grandiflorum* 'Rubrum', red flax, page 75, with its vibrant red flowers.

**Planting & Care**—Sow seed in the early fall in premoistened soil prepared without amendments. Cover seed with a light raking. Well-draining soils such as sand, loam or even gravelly soil are ideal. Don't allow seedbed to dry out at any time. In windy areas, seeds of spent flowers may drift beyond your garden, so reseeding may be necessary. All plantings respond to minimum moisture after plants are established. Avoid crowding young plants with other wildflowers; thin other species away from the plant's main stem.

*Orthocarpus purpurascens*

Right: *Nepeta x faassenii,* catmint, with yellow-flowering *Achillea* species.

Below: *Orthocarpus purpurascens,* owl's clover, blooms early in spring. Effective tucked into out-of-the-way places.

Below right: *Nemophila menziesii,* baby-blue-eyes, is a California native with striking blue flowers.

*Oenothera* species, primrose, are easy-to-grow annuals and perennials that spread by underground runners to quickly colonize an area. Here an untended planting helps reclaim an abandoned gas station.

*Oenothera berlandieri,* Mexican evening primrose, flowers from late spring into summer with rose-pink flowers on stems 10 to 12 inches high. Plants can be invasive and often overgrow smaller, less-aggressive plants.

*Papaver nudicaule*

*Penstemon eatonii*

## Papaver — Iceland Poppy, Oriental Poppy, Shirley Poppy

*Papaver nudicaule,* Iceland poppy, is a real eye-catcher with its intensely colored flowers. This perennial is native to Arctic North America but performs well in the arid West. Plants grow 1-1/2 to 3 feet high, the tall, slender stems topped with nodding, crepe-paperlike flowers to 3 inches wide. Native plants produce true orange flowers. Other flower colors available include yellow-orange, orange-red and pink. The flowering period extends from spring into summer depending on elevation and extent of heat. Leaves are sparse and divided. All plant parts are poisonous.

The tissuelike flowers of *P. orientale,* Oriental poppy, provide brilliant splashes of color early in the season. They bloom the same time as iris. When placed together they create dramatic displays. In fall plants form a basal rosette of hairy, lobed leaves that live over winter, then send up flowering stems 2 to 4 feet high. After flowering the plants go dormant, disappearing completely from mid-July until September. Flowers come in shades of red, orange, pink and white and can be 6 inches or more across. Excellent as cut flowers. Sear end of stem with flame after cutting and place immediately in water for longest-lasting bouquets.

*P. rhoeas,* Shirley poppy, is an annual that grows rapidly to 2 to 4 feet high. Large, 2-inch, single to double flowers bloom in mid- to late spring. They come in an array of bright colors: pink, white, red, orange, salmon and bicolors. Use in the background of the border or interplant among shrubs.

**Planting & Care**—Selected varieties are generally available in containers at nurseries. Or sow seed in spring in cold-winter areas. In mild-winter areas, plant seed in fall to grow as annuals. Seeds are tiny, so mix with fine sand to help determine seeding coverage. Do not rake into soil. Sprinkle gently to avoid washing out the tiny seeds. Locate in full sun or partial shade in well-prepared garden soil.

## Penstemon — Beardtongue, Penstemon

The more than 250 *Penstemon* species have four things in common: perennial growth, tubular flowers that hummingbirds enjoy, spring and early summer bloom periods and a low water requirement. Basal growth supports the numerous, tall flowering stalks. Plants tend to improve with age. In the second season, growth is more vigorous. Cut back old, dead flower stalks in late fall. Remove seeds from stems and scatter where you want new plants the next year.

The *Penstemon* species listed here represent only a small selection of those that are more readily available.

*P. barbatus,* scarlet bugler, is available in a range of sizes and flower colors. Look for 'Prairie Fire', orange-red flowers from midsummer to frost on 1- to 2-foot plants; 'Rose Elf' has clear pink flowers.
*P. eatonii,* firecracker penstemon, is a superior species with long, narrow, scarlet flowers supported by 2-foot-high stems.

*P. heterophyllus purdyi* 'Blue Bedder' has rose-lavender to blue flowers. Plants grow 1 to 2 feet high and as wide. Bloom period is April into July. Best along coast and in inland valleys.
*P. palmeri,* pink wild snapdragon, develops flower spikes to 6 feet high. Large white blossoms are tinged with lilac or pink. Blooms in early summer.
*P. parryi,* Parry's penstemon, flowers in early spring. It is an exceptional species with spikes to 2 feet high that are topped with profuse numbers of pink tubular blooms.
*P. wrightii,* a native of Texas, is similar to *P. parryi,* but its flower color is a unique, intense, pinkish red.

**Planting & Care**—Start from seed or plant from containers in fall or early spring. If sowing seed, cold-stratify for 4 to 6 weeks prior to spring seeding. (See page 118.) Prepare seedbeds well but go easy on soil amendments. Most require well-draining, loose, gravelly soils. Sow 1/4 inch deep and tamp soil. Plants need space to develop properly.

## Petalostemon purpureum — Purple Prairie Clover

The bright red and purple flower spikes of purple prairie clover are similar to those of coneflower, *Echinacea*, page 58. Orange-gold anthers of the flowers add a dramatic flair. Plants are perennial and grow 2 to 3 feet high, with elongated leaves along stems. Flowers appear along the stems and tips and bloom most profusely during the summer months.

Plants produce deep roots, making them well adapted to low-rainfall areas of the West. Growth is similar to that of white clover when plants are young, but mature plants are less aggressive. Use in the natural garden as a ground cover or on slopes for erosion control.

**Planting & Care**—Sow seed 1/16 inch deep in fall months for spring growth and to take advantage of winter rains. Seed can actually be sown any time if provided with regular moisture. Soaking them in hot water for a few hours tends to improve germination. See page 118. Premoisten soil to at least 6 inches deep prior to planting to promote the plant's deep-rooting growth. Does best in full sun. Plant in either sandy or heavy soils, as long as soil is well draining. Once established, plants are vigorous and will persist. Cut back in late fall to renew growth for the following spring. Rabbits seem to avoid eating this plant.

Native to the Great Plains

Perennial; blooms late spring to fall

Grows to 3 feet high, spreads 1-1/2 to 2 feet wide

Accepts a wide variety of well-draining soils, from sandy to heavy soils; prefers light soils

Low water use

Plant in full sun

Seeding rates: 10 grams per 100 sq. ft.; 3 ounces per 500 sq. ft.; 8 pounds per acre

*Petalostemon purpureum*

## Phacelia — California Bluebell, Lacy Phacelia

*Phacelia campanularia*, California bluebell, is a prolific and attractive annual with brilliant, royal purple or deep blue, bell-shaped flowers. Abundant, lush, dark green, fragrant, heart-shaped leaves with irregular edges provide a lush background for the flowers that blanket each plant. Range is the Pacific Northwest, Southwest deserts, Texas and Oklahoma.

Use for early spring flowers in borders with pansies as a mass planting and in wildflower mixes. It is also a colorful companion with California poppy, *Eschscholzia californica*. Their height makes *Phacelia* ideal for foreground plantings; it's also effective in rock gardens and containers. When heat arrives and flowering has ceased, the plants just seem to disappear.

*P. tanacetifolia*, lacy phacelia, produces graceful, deeply divided leaves. These 2- to 3-foot plants provide a fernlike background for dense-branching stems that are covered with clusters of lavender or blue flowers. Blooms through summer. Vigorous and aggressive growth competes well with grasses in field plantings. Prefers sunny locations below 4,000 feet. Native to valley regions from central California south to Arizona.

**Planting & Care**—Sow seed in place in fall in mild-winter areas. In cold-winter regions, wait until spring after last frost has passed. Premoisten soil prior to seeding. Sandy soil is preferred. Rake seed into soil lightly. Thin seedlings 8 to 12 inches apart to allow for spread. When given deep irrigations, growth and flowering can be extended into early summer. Avoid touching leaves; some people react with an itchy rash.

Native to central California valleys, the Mojave and Colorado deserts of California

Annual; blooms early spring to early summer

Grows less than 1 foot to 2 feet high, spreads to 1 foot wide

Provide with most any well-draining soil

Low water use

Plant in full sun

Seeding rates: 3 grams per 100 sq. ft.; 1 ounce per 500 sq. ft.; 3 pounds per acre

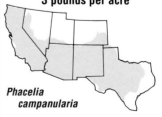

*Phacelia campanularia*

## Phlox

**Native to south central Texas**

---

**Annual; blooms late spring to early summer inland, longer near coast**

---

**Grows 6 inches to 5 feet high, spreads 1 to 2 feet wide**

---

**Provide with light, rich, well-draining soil**

---

**Moderate water use**

---

**Plant in full sun; afternoon shade will extend flowering period**

---

**Seeding rates: 10 grams per 100 sq. ft.; 3 ounces per 500 sq. ft.; 10 pounds per acre**

*Phlox drummondii*

About 60 species of phlox are native to North America. Their landscape uses are almost as numerous. They can be included in wildflower mixes, rock gardens, garden borders with other annuals or perennials, and in open fields. They are excellent in mass plantings for large areas or among shrubs or perennials in small spaces.

*P. drummondii* is an annual native to central Texas and well adapted to all regions of the arid West. Flowers in pastel shades of red, pink, white, peach or lavender are formed in clusters above light green, leafy, sticky stems. Plants grow 6 to 18 inches high with a similar spread. A location in full sun is important—growth is rangy in shade. In mild climates, flowers can last into fall. In hot, dry regions, plants grown from fall seedings often flower until early summer.

*P. glabriflora*, Rio Grande phlox, grows to 10 inches high, spreading to 18 inches wide. Flowers are deep pink with white eyes to 1 inch across and bloom in late spring. Well-draining soil is necessary; coarse sand is ideal. Native to Texas.

*P. maculata* has smaller flowerheads than *P. paniculata*, following, but plants are mildew-resistant. 'Miss Lingard', white flowers, is an old favorite that flowers in June and July. It is sometimes sold as *P. carolina*.

*P. paniculata* produces large number of fragrant flowers in red, lavender and pink from mid- to late summer. Many types have a darker or contrasting eye at the center of the blossom. Plants grow 3 to 5 feet high and should be divided every 2 to 3 years.

**Planting & Care**—Sow seed in fall in mild-winter areas. In cold climates sow in spring after danger of frost has passed. Cover seed with at least 1/2 inch of soil; darkness is required for germination. Light, rich, well-draining soil is required for heavy flower production. Regular watering during the growing season helps flowering. After first flush of bloom trim one-third of plant to stimulate new growth and more flowering.

## Physostegia virginiana

**Native to North America**

---

**Perennial; blooms early summer to early fall**

---

**Grows 2 to 4 feet high, spreads 2 to 3 feet wide**

---

**Provide with most any soil**

---

**Low to moderate water use in well-prepared soil**

---

**Plant in full sun to partial shade**

---

**Seeding rates: 12 grams per 100 sq. ft.; 4 ounces per 500 sq. ft.**

*Physostegia virginiana*

False dragonhead is an aggressive plant useful in garden borders, as a tall background or in field plantings. It relates best with old-fashioned perennial favorites such as shasta daisy, Swan River daisy, coreopsis and foxglove. Adapted to all areas from California to Texas.

This perennial can be identified by its square stems and long, opposite, 3- to 5-inch, toothed leaves. The vigorous and productive growth produces stems 3 to 4 feet high topped with 1-inch, funnel-shaped flowers in white, pink or lavender. Flowering season is from early summer to early fall. Two low-growing varieties are 'Vivid', pink flowers, and 'Summer Snow', a prolific white form that grows about 2 feet high. This size is ideal for the middle foreground in planting beds.

*P. pulchella*, beautiful false dragonhead, is a Texas native that is similar in appearance with square stems and opposite leaves. It grows to about 3 feet high and blooms in late spring.

**Planting & Care**—Sow seed in fall or spring in sun or partial shade. Sow 1/4 inch deep and tamp gently into soil. Thin seedlings 12 to 15 inches apart. Accepts almost any soil. Start new plants by dividing clumps in the fall or plant from containers available at some nurseries. Plants set seed readily and self-sow. As plants mature, they can become invasive in flower borders, so be prepared to control spreading growth or stake rangy plants. After flowering season has passed, cut back old stems and thin out excessive stolon growth to reduce crowding. Replant pruned stolons in other garden locations or give to friends.

Far left: *Papaver nudicaule,* Iceland poppy, is a perennial wildflower native to Arctic North America but one that performs well in the arid West. The crepe-paperlike flowers grow to 3 inches wide.

Left: *Phacelia campanularia,* California bluebell, is a prolific and attractive annual with brilliant, royal purple or deep blue, bell-shaped flowers.

Below left: *Phlox drummondii* is an annual native to central Texas and well adapted to all regions of the arid West.

Below: *Physostegia virginiana,* false dragonhead, grows 3 to 4 feet high, with stems topped with funnel-shaped flowers in white, pink or lavender. Flowering season is from early summer to early fall.

*Gallery of Wildflowers* ■ 93

*Psilostrophe cooperi*

*Ratibida columnifera*

## Psilostrophe — Paperflower

Paperflower shows off its refreshing flowers over a long period from spring to fall and often year-round. Miniature, yellow, sunflowerlike blooms 1 inch wide cover the low, 1-1/2- to 2-foot, mounding plants. Basal branch growth is dense but with sparse foliage. Flowers practically blanket plants during periods of peak bloom.

*Psilostrophe cooperi* is native to Utah, western New Mexico, Arizona, Southern California and northwest Mexico. Plants are naturally adapted to hot, low-rainfall regions. In the deserts of the Southwest, paperflower goes largely unnoticed and deserves wider garden use. It is worth noting that when plants are allowed to dry out for several months and then watered deeply, masses of flowers come on for another show of color. *P. tagetina*, Texas paperflower, may be less well known than *P. cooperi*, but it is blessed with a long flowering season from summer through late fall. The well-rounded, 1-1/2- to 2-foot plants are literally covered with 1-inch yellow flowers. Moderate water will maintain plants through the long flowering season. A deep taproot gives plants an increased water supply during periods without irrigation. When flowers are at the papery white or tan stage, you can cut and use them as long-lasting dried flowers.

Either species is effective as a low foreground or border plant. They blend well with wildflower plantings and with gray-foliaged plants, requiring low water applications and little maintenance.

**Planting & Care**—Seeds germinate readily. Sow seed 1/2 inch deep in premoistened soil. Plants, especially *P. cooperi*, are sometimes available in containers at specialty nurseries. Plant in full sun in well-draining soil. Seed-grown plants may take a year or so to flower. After each blooming period and when flowers have faded to a tan, papery texture, shear them off to stimulate growth of new flowering stems.

## Ratibida columnifera — Mexican Hat

(Also known as *Ratibida columnaris*.)

Mexican hat is admired for its unique flower form that resembles the broad-brimmed, high-centered hat worn during Mexican fiestas. Yellow petals drape downward, surrounding darker-colored, 1- to 2-inch, cylindrical cones. Red Mexican hat petals are mahogany-red outlined in yellow. See photo, page 16.

Growth is perennial to 3 feet high. Branches emerge from plant base and are covered with finely divided leaves. Flowers are profuse and appear during summer and into fall. The plant's deep taproot also helps control soil erosion.

Mexican hat grows naturally on gentle slopes and can often be seen along highways and in meadows in the Midwest and on Texas prairies and plains west to Arizona. Competes well with grasses. Use it as a background plant in flower borders and along fences or walls. It is also a captivating flower in mixed bouquets.

**Planting & Care**—Seeds can be sown in fall or spring and germinate quickly. Sow 1/4 to 1/2 inch deep. Plant when soil is warm and air temperature is cool. Thin seedlings to 1-1/2 feet apart to allow for spread. Cut back mature plants after seeds have dispersed in the fall. Flowers are more numerous the second season after planting. Does well in poor soils, but good drainage is required. Water needs are moderate. Too much water, especially in shady locations, can create problems with mildew and can shorten the plant's life.

# Romneya coulteri
## Matilija Poppy

Matilija poppy is certainly one of the most spectacular and cherished of all native California plants. Its natural habitats provide clues to preferred culture in garden areas: canyon beds and sandy washes in coastal California from Santa Barbara County south to San Diego County and Baja California at elevations from near sea level to 2,000 feet.

Plants are vigorous, woody-based perennials, growing 6 to 8 feet high and spreading 8 to 10 feet wide. Due to their size and rough-hewn good looks, they are not recommended for the small garden or for regular close-up viewing. However, in larger areas on slopes and on deep lots, a distant view of the immense, crepelike flowers that grow 4 to 9 inches across is something to behold. Flowers bloom most abundantly in early to midsummer, then after a short summer vacation bloom again in the fall. This varies according to location. High moisture content of plants makes them fire-retardant.

**Planting & Care**—Plants are usually available in containers at specialized nurseries. They are difficult to start from seed. Plants will not tolerate soggy or poorly drained soil. Water use is low after plants are established. Plants can become unsightly after bloom period. Cut back to near ground level in the late fall for vigorous regrowth. The most efficient propagation method is to remove suckers from older plants and replant. Or take 2-1/2-inch-long root cuttings in November or December. Plant cuttings in a mix of well-moistened and blended loam, peat moss and leaf mold. Place cuttings in the soil in horizontal position. Surround with sand to provide drainage.

*Romneya coulteri*

# Rudbeckia hirta
## Black-Eyed Susan, Gloriosa Daisy

Black-eyed Susan is a cheerful, biennial wildflower, blooming from early summer to frost. Native species have yellow-orange, 2- to 4-inch flowers with brown centers that appear on upright, branching plants 2 to 4 feet high. Leaves and stems have a rough, hairy appearance. If you cut flowers often for bouquets, plants respond by producing more flowers. The natural range for the species extends from the Rocky Mountains eastward, but it is well adapted to warm climate regions throughout the arid West.

Many selections are available in shades of yellow, orange, even russet and mahogany. All have vigorous growth comparable to the native species. Landscape uses include mass plantings in fields and on slopes and to renew disturbed sites. In the garden, plant in clusters in the back of flowerbeds and along walls or fences.

*Rudbeckia hirta*, black-eyed Susan, gloriosa daisy, begins forming buds for its summer and late-fall flowering season at the same time many other perennials are ending their flower show. However, plants have been known to bloom early in spring in frost-free areas when grown in a warm microclimate. Flowers are 5 to 7 inches across, in bright yellow, orange and russet. Plants grow 3 to 4 feet high. Two smaller selections can be used in foreground plantings: 'Marmalade', to 2 feet high, and 'Goldilocks', 1-1/2 feet high.

**Planting & Care**—Sow seed in fall for flowers the next summer. Sow 1/4 inch deep, lightly tamping seed into soil. Seedlings can be transplanted if they come up too thickly, but do this only in cool weather. Performs well in light, heavy, rich or sterile soils. Full sun is best; too much shade causes open, rangy growth. Thin plants to 2 to 3 feet apart. Water requirements are low to moderate, but do not overwater. In extremely hot weather water plants deeply to prolong flowering season. After flowering has ceased, cut back spent growth.

*Rudbeckia hirta*

Above: *Penstemon eatonii,* firecracker penstemon, is a superior species with long, narrow, scarlet flowers supported by 2-foot-high stems. Adapted throughout the arid West.

Above right: *Penstemon parryi,* Parry's penstemon, flowers in early spring. It is another exceptional penstemon with spikes to 2 feet high topped with profuse numbers of pink tubular blooms.

*Psilostrophe cooperi,* paperflower, is native to Utah, western New Mexico, Arizona, Southern California and northwest Mexico. It is one plant that deserves wider use in the Southwest deserts.

*Romneya coulteri,* matilija poppy, is one of the most valued California native plants. The striking white flowers with yellow centers can grow up to several inches across.

*Rudbeckia hirta,* black-eyed Susan, begins blooming in summer then ceases with the first fall frost. The natural range for the species extends from the Rocky Mountains eastward, but plants are well adapted to warm climates throughout the arid West.

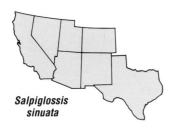

*Salpiglossis sinuata*

*Salvia columbariae*

## Salpiglossis sinuata — Painted-Tongue

The dwarf growth, vigor and wealth of color provided by painted-tongue make it an exuberant addition to any summer garden. This annual produces open, upright growth 2 to 3 feet high, supporting five-lobed flowers that look like petunias. The 4-inch, narrow, oblong green leaves and stems are sticky. Plants can be dramatic when massed in flower beds in the middle background, or in containers and bouquets.

Flower colors include yellow, purple, pink, reddish orange and mahogany-red. In addition, flower petals have striped venations for added interest. 'Bolero F2 Mixed' grows 1-1/2 to 2 feet high. 'Kew Blue' grows to just 1 foot high. 'Gloomy Rival' grows to 15 inches high. Its pearl gray flowers with rich bronze veins are the perfect complement to silver- or gray-leaved plants.

**Planting & Care**—Seeds are quite small, so mix with fine sand and sow on soil surface. Seeds can be slow to germinate in open areas, but you can start them indoors in small pots in early spring and transplant seedlings after danger of frost has passed and seedlings are well rooted. Space plants 1 to 1-1/2 feet apart to allow for adequate growth. Locate in sunny locations in soil that has been enriched with organic matter. Unlike for most wildflowers, adding a balanced fertilizer to the soil also assists growth. Well-draining soil is important. Avoid watering from overhead sprinklers. Best method is to flood irrigate deeply to develop a deep root system. Do not overwater. Thin branches in mid-season to encourage renewal of flowering wood.

## Salvia — Scarlet Sage

The flowers of *Salvia* species seem to have a special brilliance. Plants also have many landscape uses—in shrub or flower borders and mass plantings. They naturalize vigorously once they're established. Hummingbirds love the flowers.

*Salvia coccinea*, scarlet sage, is native to Texas. It produces 3/4- to 1-inch flowers that are clustered in spikes on stems to 2 feet tall. Deep green, heart-shaped leaves provide a lush, vigorous appearance during the summer and fall months. 'Lady in Red', a recent All-America Selections award winner, grows 12 to 15 inches high with bright red flowers.

*S. columbariae*, chia, is widely adapted throughout California and the Southwest. Plants grow 1 to 1-1/2 feet high with vertical stems that hold blue flower clusters, one above the other, in flower cups. Flowers bloom in spring. They are excellent in combination with California poppy. The seeds of chia are edible and were harvested by Native Americans in California and Mexico. *S. farinacea*, mealy cup sage, is a popular and colorful annual grown in cold climates, a perennial elsewhere. It grows rapidly to form a clump 2 to 3 feet high. Violet-blue flowers develop along gray-green stems. Highly attractive when planted in combination with scarlet sage and *S. greggii*, red salvia. Native to Texas and New Mexico.

**Planting & Care**—Plant from containers in fall or spring, or start from seed sown in place. Sow seed 1/16 inch deep. Thin seedlings to 12 inches apart. Grows best in well-draining, sandy or loam soils. Sunny locations are ideal. Reseeds in abundance. Remove spent flower spikes after frost and in midseason to stimulate production of more flowers. Water needs are low to moderate after plants are established. In low-rainfall areas, extra moisture will increase vigor.

# Silene

## Catchfly, Sweet William Catchfly

For deep pink flowers during summer, consider planting the colorful annual *Silene armeria*. Its common name, catchfly, refers to the sticky sap the plant produces that captures and holds small insects. Introduced from southern Europe, catchfly has now naturalized in North America. It is well adapted for use in rock gardens, mass plantings, garden borders and wildflower mixes. Light green, basal leaves to 3 inches long wither early as flowering develops, but they are followed by the profuse, flat-topped clusters of rose pink, 1-inch flowers that blanket the 1- to 2-foot plant. The selection 'Dwarf' grows to a dainty and compact 8 inches high.

*S. californica*, California indian pink, is a perennial native to foothill regions in California. Plant form is loose and open, reaching 6 to 16 inches high. Flowers to 1-1/2 inches wide are flaming red and put on a show during spring. Plants require a well-draining soil.

*S. laciniata*, Indian pink, grows to 1 foot high with reddish orange flowers that bloom in summer, after *S. californica*.

**Planting & Care**—Plants are easy to grow and are not fussy about their growing conditions. As mentioned, *S. californica* requires well-draining soil. Plant seed in the fall or spring, sowing on soil surface, pressing into soil to ensure good contact. Fall-sown seeds often produce flowers the following growing season. Accepts low to moderate moisture in heavy to light soils. Does well in full sun to partial shade.

Native to Europe and California

———

Annual and perennial; blooms late spring into summer

———

Grows 6 inches to 2 feet high, spreads 12 to 15 inches wide

———

Provide with light to heavy soils but should have good drainage

———

Low to moderate water use

———

Plant in full sun to partial shade

———

Seeding rates: 3 grams per 100 sq. ft.; .5 ounces per 500 sq. ft.; 1 pound per acre

*Silene armeria*

# Sisyrinchium bellum

## California Blue-Eyed Grass

California blue-eyed grass is a perennial wildflower grown for its distinctive, irislike leaves and dainty, silky, blue flowers with yellow eyes. It grows 6 to 16 inches high. The upright form and narrow spread make it ideal for tucking into rock gardens and among large boulders. Flowers bloom during the spring and summer months. Although individual flowers last only one day, new flowers open daily and continue for many months. In Texas, its bloom season is often the same as that of iris.

Blue-eyed grass is native to California's coastal meadows and oak woodlands. The range of adaptability stretches from Canada to the Rocky Mountains and the Southwest. Also consider growing a similar yellow-flowering species, *S. californicum*.

Plant in clusters for accents or in naturalized areas and wildflower meadows. Grasslike growth blends well with low-growing grasses, bulbs and small wildflowers. *Dietes vegeta*, fortnight lily, is an excellent companion plant due to its similar size, flower form and upright growth habit.

**Planting & Care**—It's important to sow seed in the fall so plants will become established before hot weather. Sow seed so it is covered by soil. Mature plants can be divided for transplanting during cooler periods. Locate in sunny areas. Moist locations are ideal if soil drains well. Accepts dry conditions after plants are established.

Native to coastal meadows and oak woodlands of California

———

Perennial; blooms early spring to early summer

———

Grows 6 to 16 inches high, spreads 12 to 18 inches wide

———

Provide with well-draining soil: sand, loam or clay

———

Low to moderate water use

———

Plant in full sun to partial shade

———

Seeding rates: 12 grams per 100 sq. ft.; 4 ounces per 500 sq. ft.; 8 pounds per acre

*Sisyrinchium bellum*

*Silene armeria,* sweet William catchfly, produces its deep pink flowers during summer. Its common name is due to the sticky sap the plant produces that captures and holds small insects.

*Salvia coccinea,* scarlet sage, is a Texas native that produces 1-inch flowers in clusters on stems to 2 feet tall. Deep green, heart-shaped leaves provide a lush appearance during the summer and fall months.

*Salpiglossis sinuata,* painted-tongue, is an vigorous-growing annual, reaching 2 to 3 feet high. The five-lobed flowers look similar to petunias, and come in a range of colors.

*Sisyrinchium bellum,* California blue-eyed grass, is grown for its distinctive, irislike leaves and dainty, silky, blue flowers with yellow eyes. Its upright form and narrow spread make it ideal for tucking into rock gardens and among large boulders.

**Native to California and Baja California**

---

**Annual; blooms late spring into summer**

---

**Grows to 2 feet high, spreads 1-1/2 feet wide**

---

**Provide with well-draining soil**

---

**Low to moderate water use**

---

**Plant in dappled tree shade or where plants will receive morning sun**

---

**Seeding rates: 16 grams per 100 sq. ft.; 2 ounces per 500 sq. ft.; 12 pounds per acre**

*Stylomecon heterophylla*

**Native to Europe, Asia and California**

---

**Perennial; blooms spring to late summer**

---

**Grows 2 to 6 feet high, spreads 3 feet wide**

---

**Provide with mositure-retentive soil improved with organic matter**

---

**Moderate to high water use**

---

**Plant in partial shade to full sun**

---

**Seeding rates: 5 grams per 100 sq. ft.; 1 ounce per 500 sq. ft.; 4 pounds per acre**

*Thalictrum aquilegifolium*

## Stylomecon heterophylla — Flaming Poppy, Wind Poppy

If you want to grow a plant with unusual flowers, flaming poppy should be on your list. Flowers are an unusual, orange to brick-red color surrounding a deep purple center. The finely divided, somewhat fleshy leaves appear on graceful stems that reach 2 feet high. Flaming poppy is native to California and Baja California, although its range of adaptation covers a large portion of western North America.

Use this summer-blooming annual in partially shaded locations as a border and at the perimeter of landscaped areas. It is also excellent for close-up viewing. Blend with other poppy species such as California poppy in clusters to create interesting color contrasts.

**Planting & Care**—Seeds germinate easily. Sow in place in the early spring months, covering with 1/16 inch of soil. Keep soil moist but do not overwater. Thin seedlings 9 to 12 inches apart to allow for natural spread and productive growth. Plants require good soil drainage. Soil that contains excessive organic matter or plants located in heavy shade can cause weak root development and spindly growth. Water needs are moderate after plants are established.

Be aware that seed may be difficult to find. Check with companies that specialize in native plants. A source list of mail-order suppliers is listed on page 111.

## Thalictrum — Meadow Rue

*Thalictrum aquilegifolium*, meadow rue, plays a special role in perennial wildflower mixes, adding a unique, airy, open feel to the scene. The 2- to 3-foot high, sparsely leaved stems and bluish green leaves resemble perennial species of columbine, *Aquilegia*. Open, fluffy, lilac or purple flowers are dramatic on tall stems.

Locate plantings at the rear of the border. Meadow rue is also effective against a dark green, shrubby background. Graceful basal foliage blends well in floral arrangements. Adapted to all areas. Provide protection in cool or windy locations. Plants are generally long-lived when located in sun or partial shade.

*T. dipterocarpum*, Chinese meadow rue, grows 3 to 6 feet high with shimmering sprays of lavender to mauve flowers accented with yellow stamens. It is an excellent long-lived perennial in the flower border and for cut flowers. Adapted to all areas.

*T. polycarpum* is a worthy California native—locate in that dry, shady spot. Attractive, lacy green leaves reach to 6 feet high. Whitish flowers appear in early spring to early summer.

**Planting & Care**—Propagate by division in early spring, set out seedlings from seed started indoors, or sow in place outdoors, covering seed with 1/8 inch of soil. Tamp to ensure good seed-to-soil contact. If soils are light or heavy, blend in organic matter. Accepts most any soil as long as it is well draining.

## Tithonia rotundifolia — Mexican Sunflower

The 3- to 4-inch, orange to yellow flower heads of Mexican sunflower provide a vigorous show of color from midsummer until frost. Plants are often grown as annuals in outlying garden areas, or in fields or meadow plantings where the robust plants have room to develop to their full, 6-foot height and width. Velvety green, hairy leaves grow as much as 1 foot long in an ovate to triangular form, producing a lush effect. Flowers attract swallowtail butterflies.

Plants are native to Mexico and Central America. They tolerate heat and drought once established—a good choice for dry gardens. Large flowers with their yellow tufted heads are prominent additions to indoor arrangements. Stems are hollow and bend easily. Cutting flowers often will help plants produce more blooms. Deadhead spent flowers as they occur.

'Goldfinger' is a smaller version, growing 2 to 2-1/2 feet high with vivid, orange-scarlet flowers to 3 inches across. Bloom begins in midsummer and continues until plants are killed by the first fall frost. 'Yellow Torch' grows 3 to 4 feet high with chrome-yellow, 2-1/2-inch blooms. It is a plant of noble proportions, excellent for cutting or in the natural border.

**Planting & Care**—Sow seed in clusters during fall where you want plants to grow. Sow 1/2 inch deep. Germination is usually rapid. Plants are well adapted to poor soils. Locate in full sun and water deeply to help roots develop. Space plants 3 feet apart to allow for the wide-spreading, robust growth. Groom plants by removing damaged leaves after first frost in fall. Reseeds easily.

Native to Mexico and Central America

Annual; blooms midsummer until first frost

Grows 2 to 6 feet high, spreads 2 to 4 feet wide

Provide with most any well-draining soil

Low water use; occasional deep watering helps produce deep roots

Plant in full sun

Seeding rates: 7 grams per 100 sq. ft.; 1.5 ounces per 500 sq. ft.; 5 pounds per acre

*Tithonia rotundifolia*

## Venidium fastuosum — Cape Daisy

The silvery green, irregularly lobed leaves of cape daisy provide a luxuriant background for the large, 5-inch, orange, sunflowerlike flowers. The brightly colored blooms have the added attraction of a blackish purple zone and dark, purple-brown base. Flower buds look like spiderwebs when young.

The mature height of cape daisy is 2 feet, which makes it effective as a background in the flower bed or in wildflower mixes. This annual's flowering season lasts from early to late summer. Combining cape daisy with early spring-blooming *Dimorphotheca sinuata*, African daisy, page 55, greatly extends the attractive qualities of the planting. This is particularly true in mild-climate, low-elevation regions. Plants are well adapted to California's San Joaquin Valley and low- and middle-elevation desert regions.

**Planting & Care**—Sow seed directly on the surface of well-prepared soil after danger of last frost has passed. Water gently to help make good seed-to-soil contact. Plants in containers are also sometimes available at nurseries. Locate planting beds in partial shade. Seeds germinate in about 10 days with 70F to 75F soil temperatures. Keep soil moist. Thin seedlings 6 to 12 inches apart to allow for dense, spreading growth.

Native to South Africa

Annual; blooms early to late summer

Grows to 2 feet high, spreads 1 to 1-1/2 feet wide

Provide with well-draining, well-prepared soil

Moderate water use

Plant in partial shade

Seeding rates: 7 grams per 100 sq. ft.; 1.5 ounces per 500 sq. ft.

*Venidium fastuosum*

*Stylomecon heterophylla,* flaming poppy, is grown for its unusual flower color: orange to brick-red surrounding a deep purple center. It is native to California and Baja California.

*Tithonia rotundifolia,* Mexican sunflower, produces 3- to 4-inch, orange to yellow flowerheads from summer until frost. Give plants plenty of space to develop to their full 6-foot height and width.

Left: *Verbena* species are workhorse, low-water-use perennials in hot, dry regions. Plants grow 6 to 9 inches high and spread 2 to 3 feet wide, which makes them excellent as ground covers.

Below left: *Verbena* are well-adapted to natural garden designs.

Below: *Venidium fastuosum,* cape daisy, grows to 2 feet high, which makes it effective as a background in the flower bed or in wildflower mixes. Combine cape daisy with early spring blooming *Dimorphotheca sinuata,* African daisy, for an extended show of flowers.

**Native to southwest U.S.**

———

**Perennial, in cold areas grow as annual; blooms early spring until heavy frost**

———

**Grows 6 inches to 2 feet high, spreads 2 to 4 feet wide**

———

**Provide with most any soil; loose, well-draining soils help increase plant vigor**

———

**Low water use**

———

**Plant in full sun, becomes straggly in shade**

———

**Seeding rates: 8 grams per 100 sq. ft.; 2 ounces per 500 sq. ft.; 6 pounds per acre**

*Verbena gooddingii*

**Native to Colorado and Kansas, south to Mexico and the U.S. Southwest**

———

**Perennial; blooms summer into fall**

———

**Grows 6 inches high, spreads 6 to 12 inches wide**

———

**Provide with well-draining soil**

———

**Low water use; overhead watering can cause mildew problems**

———

**Plant in full sun to partial shade**

———

**Seeding rates: 12 grams per 100 sq. ft.; 4 ounces per 500 sq. ft.**

*Zinnia grandiflora*

# Verbena

### Verbena

*Verbena* species work well as mixed colors blended together or as solid plantings of a single color. They are low-water-use perennials that produce profuse numbers of short-spiked, tufted flowers. All verbena are persistent and vigorous growers. Plants grow 6 to 9 inches high and spread 2 to 3 feet wide, making them excellent as ground covers. In cold-winter areas, most profuse flowering occurs during hot summer months. In warm climates, plants bloom throughout the year, although a severe frost usually puts an end to flowering.

*V. gooddingii* is native to Arizona and California's eastern Mojave Desert and is widely adapted throughout the West. It is superior as a foreground cover, its pinkish lavender flowers brightening the bases of low-growing shrubs, narrow dividers, rock gardens among boulders and natural landscapes. Perennial growth makes it useful to sow on slopes for erosion control, blended with other seeded wildflowers. Plants grow to 2 feet high and spread to 4 feet wide.

*V. peruviana* has flat-topped flowers in red, pink, lavender and purple that literally cover the small, neat leaves. It is cold-hardy to 28F and a favorite color plant in warm desert and inland valley regions. Select from many hybrids, with pink, red, white and purple flower colors available.

*V. tenuisecta*, moss verbena, is a similar favorite perennial, its branches covered with clusters of lavender to purple flowers from early spring to fall. The finely divided, deep green leaves create a thick, ground-hugging mat to 1 foot high. Some dormancy occurs during high heat. Cut back severely with nylon line trimmer in winter after plants become dormant to encourage new growth.

**Planting & Care**—Plant from containers in fall or spring, or sow seed of *V. tenuisecta* 1/16 inch deep in spring as weather begins to warm, tamping in place. Overwatering can reduce flowering. Plants can be aggressive and outgrow their boundaries—trim to control. Plants also reseed readily.

# Zinnia grandiflora

### Prairie Zinnia

Prairie zinnia is a perennial well adapted to natural garden designs. It has a low, ground-hugging habit and produces many orange-yellow flowers that are borne at the same level, creating a carpet of color. Flowers are 1 to 1-1/2 inches across and bloom from summer into fall. The slender, deep green leaves grow to form a mossy mat.

Prairie zinnia is native to Colorado and Kansas south to Mexico and the American Southwest. It is adapted to most areas of the U.S. as long as humidity is not too high. Use in a mass planting, on slopes for a rapid cover or in the natural border.

**Planting & Care**—Sow seed in place 1/4 inch deep in early spring. Seeds germinate rapidly in warm weather. Thin plants to 1 foot apart to allow for spread. As with other zinnias, do not water from overhead sprinklers or mildew problems can result. Apply water beneath foliage. Do this by flood-irrigating, which also helps

water reach deeply into the soil. Grows best in full sun. Becomes drought-tolerant after plants are established. Providing intermittent water in summer extends the flowering period. During winter, plants become dormant and practically disappear. Cut back to basal growth and plants will regrow as their rhizomes spread underground.

# Other Worthy Wildflowers

Here are more than a dozen genera of *worthy wildflowers*—flowering plants that have unusual characteristics or adaptations. Some, perhaps, could have been included in the preceding encyclopedic listing but may not be as available or as widely adapted. Unless otherwise noted, seed can often be purchased from mail-order sources. We think you'll find these wildflowers interesting and hope you can find room in your garden for a few of them.

## Abronia villosa
### Sand Verbena
**Native to sand dunes of desert Southwest**

When fall and winter rainfall are adequate, *Abronia villosa,* sand verbena, arrives on schedule in desert areas, making its appearance during the winter to early spring months. Plants are annuals and can be seen in the wild in sand dunes and other sandy locales in the Mojave Desert, southwestern Arizona and north to Utah. Profuse numbers of rose to purple flowers cover the plant, making the sandy slopes and hillsides come alive with color. Although it is not a true *Verbena,* the flowers look much like those of *Verbena* species. Leaves and stems are hairy and sticky. *A. villosa* is adapted to hot, sunny regions and prefers well-draining, sandy soil. Along the coast north of Orange County, California, look for the similar *A. umbellata,* a perennial with rosy pink flowers.

## Argemone platyceras
### Prickly Poppy
**Native to Southwest desert areas**

At first glance, the immense, 4-inch, white, crinkly flowers with the bright yellow stamens look like the favorite California native, *Romneya coulteri,* matilija poppy. Prickly poppy actually has a wider range, thriving in hot, dry locations throughout Texas, Arizona and Southern California, while matilija poppy is best adapted to cooler coastal regions. Plants grow to 3 feet high; the coarse, gray-green leaves, stems and flower buds are covered with thistlelike thorns. Flowers are most prolific in spring and summer and can bloom throughout warm periods of the year.

This is a plant to be viewed from a distance. It will accept the most inhospitable conditions, such as dry, sunny locations at the perimeter of the landscape. It often naturalizes in disturbed areas. Easy to start from seed sown in fall. All parts of the plant are poisonous.

## Aristida purpurea
### Purple Threeawn Grass
**Native to the Southwest , Colorado, Kansas and Arkansas**

This is one of the most colorful of the small ornamental grasses. It provides a unique textured effect among desert plants such as ocotillo, yuccas and low-growing flowering wildflowers. It is now being used commercially such as in golf course developments to control soil erosion on slopes. Plants are tufted with a grassy appearance, growing 18 inches high and as wide. The nodding seedheads are about 6 inches high, and are easily identified due to their purplish color. They develop from April through October. Leaf blades are 2 to 6 inches long and 1/8 inch wide. Grows in sandy soils from 1,000 to 5,000 elevation. Prefers full sun. Hardy to 10F. Keep plants looking fresh by cutting back growth to near ground level April to May.

## Bupleurum rotundifolium
### 'Green Gold'
**Native to Europe**

This plant looks like a *Euphorbia,* has leaves like a eucalyptus, and has special flowers and colors as well as an unusual plant form. Flower umbels have a chartreuse tint; flowers are 1 inch across with yellow centers. Growth is shrubby and branching to 2 feet high. Stems flow through ovate leaves 1-1/2 inch long that contrast nicely with the reddish stems.

Grows well in borders or open areas in sun or in moderately shaded areas. Unique flowers add interest for close-up viewing in containers. Plants naturalize readily in the open. Abundant growth in late spring and summer yields material for cutting for indoor arrangements. Sow seed in the spring. Germination is rapid, and plants are well adapted to dry, sterile soils and warm-climate regions. In mild-winter areas, it can be grown as a perennial.

*C. neomexicana,* with pink to purple flowers during spring to late summer. In Texas, *C. undulatum* is the species of note; it blooms during fall. All are low water users and require little care except cutting back in early winter for renewed growth the following spring.

## Collinsia heterophylla
### Chinese Houses
**Native to California**

Chinese houses is an annual wildflower that produces fascinating white and lavender, bicolored flowers that look like snapdragon blossoms balanced on tiers. Upper petals are white; lower petals are lavender. Flowering season is from spring into summer. Triangular, light green leaves are widely spaced on stems. Plants grow to 2 feet high and are dainty enough to combine with bulbs or in a blended mix of low-growing annuals. The flowers with their pagodalike tiers create fascinating cut flower arrangements.

Sow seed in fall or spring. Cover by shallow raking or apply a light, organic material over soil surface. Seeds germinate within two weeks if temperature and moisture are ideal—70F. Chinese houses reseeds easily.

## Datura
### Sacred Datura, Angel's Trumpet, Jimson Weed
**Native to North America**

Gardeners and nongardeners alike are probably familiar with the distinctive flowers of *Datura* species, a common roadside wildflower that often pops up in disturbed soil. *D. wrightii* is one of the most common species found in the Southwest. *D. discolor* is also common and is often seen in desert washes in Arizona and Southern California. It blooms earlier than *D. wrightii.* The trumpet-shaped flowers are white to pale lavender. The numerous 6-inch flowers extend above the rough, gray-green leaves from late spring until the

first killing frost. Plants can develop into mounds to 2-1/2 feet high or more. Easy to grow from seed. Be aware, however, that plant parts are highly poisonous. Indian tribes used plants with great caution as a hallucinogen, particularly by boys as a rite of passage into manhood.

## Erigeron divergens
### Fleabane Daisy
**Native to western North America**

Fleabane daisy blends well in the natural garden when combined with other wildflowers. Its long bloom period extends flowering after other more dramatic-blooming wildflowers have faded away. Plants grow to 18 inches high with an equal spread. If plants receive adequate moisture the white, daisylike flowers bloom from April until the first frost. In nature plants grow at elevations of 1,000 feet up to 9,000 feet, and are not fussy as to soil type.

## Hyptis emoryi
### Desert Lavender
**Native to southern Arizona, Sonoran Desert in Southern California**

Desert lavender is at home at elevations below 3,000 feet in California's Colorado Desert and the southern Mojave Desert. Plants grow erect with gray, woolly, aromatic leaves. Size can vary from 3 to 10 feet high. The small violet flowers bloom late winter to late spring. During this time, bees visit in abundance. Desert lavender is excellent in the background, setting the stage for more colorful and smaller-stature wildflowers. Prune lightly to maintain form after flowers have ceased. Plants are sometimes available in containers at nurseries.

## Kallstroemia grandiflora
### Arizona Poppy, Caltrop
**Native to Arizona, Texas and Mexico**

During late spring and summer, Arizona poppy puts on a most colorful show with its bright orange flowers that are highlighted with red centers. Flowers resemble those of *Eschscholzia californica,* California poppy, except that they have five petals instead of four. Growth is open and sprawling, with a spread to 4 feet wide and 1 foot

Above left: *Argemone platyceras,* prickly poppy, grows to 3 feet high; the coarse, gray-green leaves, stems and flower buds are covered with thistlelike thorns. Flowers are most prolific in spring and summer.

Above: *Stachys coccinea,* betony, grows to 2 feet high or more. Hummingbirds are attracted to the bright red, tubular flowers that bloom in spring and fall.

Left: *Zinnia grandiflora,* prairie zinnia, is a low, ground-hugging plant, producing profuse numbers of orange-yellow flowers to create a carpet of color. Flowers bloom from summer into fall.

high. Flowers bloom from late spring through summer. However, in their native environment they respond best during the summer rainy season, which occurs throughout the Sonoran Desert in southern Arizona. Note that seeds can be difficult to germinate. Sow additional seeds to help get enough plants started.

## Nicotiana alata
### Jasmine Tobacco
**Native to South America**

This perennial species is well known for its fragrant, white, summer flowers that open at night and on cloudy days. The 5-pointed lobes at the end of the 2- to 4-inch deep-throated flower produce a multi-flowered effect. Large, 4- to 6-inch, sticky, ovate leaves cover the 2- to 3-foot stems. Plant in sun or partial shade. Generally grown as an annual due to sensitivity to frost. Can be grown throughout the U.S. when planted after frost. In temperate climates plants may persist with protection. Tall growth provides good background display in flower borders. Plants tolerate heat but need adequate moisture for long flower production.

## Sphaeralcea
### Globe Mallow
**Native to deserts of U.S. Southwest**

Mallows produce a wide range of flower colors, from white to pale yellow, lavender, apricot, pink, red and orange. In Arizona and California desert regions, *Sphaeralcea ambigua,* apricot mallow, blooms in late winter to late spring. In New Mexico and Texas, *S. angustifolia lobata,* lobeleaf copper mallow, blooms late summer through fall. Each plant has its own color. Plants grow 3 to 4 feet high and 2 to 3 feet wide. *S. incana,* scarlet globe mallow, resembles small hollyhocks with bright, red-orange flowers on stems 3 to 5 feet high.

Mallows are good plants to combine with perennial and annual wild-flowers—they'll provide color during late spring and early summer when the bloom periods of many wildflowers are winding down. In addition, the gray-green foliage blends well with many other desert plants. Plants are easy to start from seed; plant almost any time.

## Stachys coccinea
### Betony, Red Mint
**Native to central Arizona, New Mexico and west Texas**

This is an easy-to-grow perennial that prefers a little more moisture than most native desert wildflowers. Betony is a plant that could be included in a mini-oasis or next to a water feature or wildlife pond. Plants grow 1 to 2 feet high, sometimes more, with bright red, tubular flowers 3/4 to 1 inch long. Hummingbirds are attracted to the flowers. Bloom period is from spring to fall, with fewer flowers during the heat of summer. Leaves are medium green to 3 inches long; the undersides covered with long hairs.

Sow seed in fall or winter. Plants accept either sun or shade, but, as mentioned, do best with regular moisture.

## Viguiera
### Golden Eye
**Native to west Texas, New Mexico, Arizona**

Golden eye is similar to the Southwest desert native *Encelia farinosa,* brittle bush. The stems are more slender, the leaves are more green than gray-green and have a less triangular shape. The plant has a rounded form and grows 3 to 6 feet high and about 3 feet wide. The yellow flowers are borne on tall stems and make long-lasting cut flowers. *Viguiera dentata,* sunflower golden eye, is native to west Texas, Arizona and New Mexico. The yellow, daisylike flowers grow to 1-1/2 inches across. *V. annua* is an annual growing to 3 feet high. Flowers to 1 inch in diameter bloom profusely during summer and into fall. *V. multiflora,* showy golden eye, grows to 3 feet high. It is best adapted to higher elevations such as those common in New Mexico.

Due to the vigorous growth of plants, cut off old flowers as they complete their cycle to encourage even more flowers. All accept a wide range of soils and growing conditions. These are low-water-use plants after they are established.

# Mail-Order Seed Sources

Southwestern Native Seeds
P.O. Box 50503
Tucson, AZ 85703
Catalog available; small fee
required.

Wild Seed, Inc.
P.O. Box 27751
Tempe, AZ 85285
(602) 276-3536
Free catalog available.

Carter Seeds
475 Mar Vista Drive
Vista, CA 92083
(619) 724-5931
Catalog available.

Clyde Robin Seed Co.
PO Box 2366
Castro Valley, CA 94546
(510) 785-0425
Catalog available.

J.L. Hudson, Seedsman
P.O. Box 1058
Redwood City, CA 94064
Catalog available; small fee
required.

Larner Seeds
P.O. Box 407
Bolinas, CA 94924
(415) 868-9407
Catalog available; small fee
required.

Theodore Payne Foundation
10459 Tuxford Street
Sun Valley, CA 91352
(818) 768-1802
Catalog available; small fee
required.

Wildflower Seed Company
Box 406
St. Helena, CA 94574
Catalog available.

Rocky Mountain Rare Plants
1706 Deerpath Road
Franktown, CO 80116-9462
Catalog available. Seeds sold Oct. 1
to March 1 only.

Western Native Seed
P.O. Box 1463
Salida, CO 81201
(719) 275-8414
Price list/catalog available; small
fee required.

Seeds Trust
High Altitude Gardens
P.O. Box 1048
Hailey, ID 83333
(208) 788-4363
Catalog available; small fee
required.

Niche Gardens
1111 Dawson Road
Chapel Hill, NC 27516-8576
(919) 967-0078
Catalog available; small fee
required. Plants only.

Desert Moon Nursery
P.O. Box 600
Veguita, NM 87062
(505) 864-0614
Catalog available; small fee
required.

Plants of the Southwest
Box 11-A
Santa Fe, NM 87501
(505) 471-2212
Catalog available; small fee
required.

W. Atlee Burpee Co.
300 Park Avenue
Warminster, PA 18974
(215) 674-4900
Catalog available.

The Antique Rose Emporium
Rt. 5 Box 143
Brenham, TX 77833
(409) 836-9051
Catalog available; small fee
required.

Douglass W. King Co., Inc.
P.O. Box 200320
San Antonio, TX 78220
(210) 661-4191
Catalog available; small fee
required.

Green Horizons
145 Scenic Hill Road
Kerrville, TX 78028
(210) 257-5141
Catalog available; send self-
addressed, stamped envelope.

Texas Seed Co., Inc.
P.O. Drawer 599
221 Airport Boulevard
Kenedy, TX 78119
(210) 583-9873
Price list/catalog available.

Wildseed Farms
P.O. Box 3000
Wildflower Hills
Fredericksburg, TX 78624
(800) 848-0078
Catalog available.

# WILDFLOWERS: THE BASICS

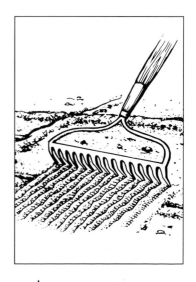

Whether you grow wildflowers along the coast, in the mountains or inland valleys, on high plains or in low-elevation, subtropical deserts, success will come by duplicating, as closely as possible, the natural environments of the wildflowers you choose to grow. Many wildflowers will grow and flower in difficult conditions, but only if they are adapted to the soil type (including drainage), moisture, heat, cold, wind, sunlight and shade you supply them. They also must be planted at the right time, with proper soil temperature, with sufficient moisture and without extreme competition from weeds.

It helps a great deal to understand the natural progression of the seasons in your region, and time planting and maintenance in tune with them. Keep records of planting dates, watering, timing and methods of weed control, when flowers bloomed and when they ceased blooming. This will help you repeat your successes and avoid duplicating most failures.

When growing wildflowers, one of the basic rules of gardening changes: fertilizing is almost always unnecessary. Adding fertilizer to most soils promotes excessive foliage growth, which reduces flower development. Exceptions are when you plant in sterile soils or when plants are in highly competitive garden situations; then additional nutrients may be required.

In any climate, seeds depend on moisture to germinate and grow. In many regions you can't count on rain to fall in sufficient amounts to supply all moisture needs. Establishing a watering schedule begins with soaking the soil to several inches deep before planting. This places moisture in the root zone area, which will act as a reservoir for future plant growth. After seeds are planted, it is important that soil moisture be maintained diligently so seeds will germinate. Any neglect in the watering program—especially if drying winds occur—can lead to disappointment.

Following these basic principles will help you bring your wildflower garden to life. With a little planning, patience and proper timing, you'll create a flower garden that'll be wildly successful.

Most wildflowers require less water after they reach flowering stage. Watering about once a week will prolong the bloom period and keep plants healthy, but varies according to your climate and seasonal conditions. Shown here are *Dimorphotheca sinuata*, African daisy.

When moistened, sandy soil crumbles and falls apart when you squeeze it in your hand.

Moist clay soil will form a ball and "ribbon" through your fingers when squeezed.

Moistened loam soil is crumbly but tends to hold together in your hands.

# Getting Ready to Plant

The first question to consider before you plant your wildflowers is: "Should I improve the soil of my planting site?" The answer to that question is "yes," "no" and "it depends." Most kinds of garden plants—annuals, vegetables, perennials, landscape trees and shrubs—grow better and healthier in a soil that has been improved with organic matter. The same is true of selected wildflowers and in certain situations. But most wildflowers are not fussy about soil. If your soil has good drainage, you can grow the great majority of plants described in this book. Those native to your region will probably do best in the natural, unimproved soil that exists on site.

Unfortunately, many housing developments today are built on *compacted soils*—those that have been excavated and moved around during construction. Your soil may be in far from a natural state, made up of subsoil instead of topsoil.

Some plants introduced from higher-rainfall regions and selected perennial wildflowers prefer soil that contains a fair portion of organic matter. Soil high in organic matter holds moisture and nutrients in the root zone longer to the benefit of most plants. Extremely fast-draining, sandy soils often benefit from the addition of organic matter, making more efficient use of the water applied.

Before you select wildflowers for your landscape, get to know your soil and determine if it will support the kinds of wildflowers you want to grow. It may be smarter to select wildflowers that will grow in the soil you have on site, rather than to attempt to modify your soil to suit particular wildflowers.

## Identifying Your Soil

Soils in the West are highly variable from one geographic region to the next, as well as from landscape to landscape on the same street. Most are low in organic matter. This is because natural vegetation is sparse in low-rainfall regions. Leaves, stems and other plant parts are not available in large quantities to decay and create organic material. The long periods of intense heat also cause organic matter to dissipate quickly.

Basic soil types include heavy *clay soils,* such as those found in coastal California, or *sandy soils* common to the desert regions of Southern California, Nevada, Arizona and New Mexico. Some regions are blessed with *loam soils,* a balanced mixture of materials relatively high in organic matter.

**Sandy soils**—These are composed of a high percentage of large particles, and water drains through quickly. Moistened sandy soil will crumble and fall apart when squeezed in your hand. In desert regions the particulates that make up sandy soil cause it to blow easily in heavy winds. Nutrients, particularly nitrogen, are *leached*— washed down from plant roots—by rapid drainage. Sandy soils absorb water at a rate of 2 inches or more per hour. They warm up more quickly in the spring than clay soils and are also the easiest to work. Plant roots develop freely in sandy soils.

**Clay soils**—Small, tightly compacted particles, heavy, dense and sticky when wet describe clay soils. If you squeeze moistened clay soil in your hand, it will "ribbon" through your fingers. Moisture moves through clay soils slowly. When you apply water, it tends to create puddles and pools rather quickly. Clay soils absorb water at a rate of less than 1/4 inch per hour. Do not dig or cultivate clay soil when it's wet, or large clods will form when the soil dries. Clay soils can develop a crusting on the surface, which repels water. Roots grow slowly and often remain shallow, spreading out horizontally.

**Loam soils**—These are ideal soils for plant growth. They are a balanced mixture of clay, sand and organic matter, and are generally well draining. Loam soil is crumbly or "friable" in your hand. Organic material in loam creates variable spaces among the soil particles, holding moisture and nutrients in the root zone longer to the benefit of plants. Loam soils absorb water at the rate of 1/4 inch to 2 inches per hour. They can crust over like clay soils, repelling water.

Granitized alluvial soils are less common. They are found at the bases of mountains and hills, fanning out due to the forces of water runoff. They are coarse, "young" soils, still in the process of breaking down from large particles to smaller ones. Alluvial soils drain well, and roots penetrate if given plenty of moisture. When dry, alluvial soils are difficult to work. These soils benefit from addition of organic matter to increase their moisture-holding capacity.

## Problem Soils

*Hardpan* is a serious problem soil in the arid West. Hardpan is generally found in heavy clay soil areas on level valley floors where the land has been farmed for long periods.

*Caliche* is a calcareous soil formed from mineral deposits that create cementlike layers—practically impenetrable if more than a few feet thick. The solution may be drastic—creating raised beds or drainage "chimneys" in planting holes with a pickaxe, power auger or post-hole digger. In fact, it's wise to check the depth and workability of the existing soil when shopping for a new home or property to avoid serious soil drainage problems.

*Saline soils* are common on converted farmlands and in many desert regions. Soils are salty due to years of irrigation to the same depth and regular use of salt-based fertilizers. Water supplied from the Colorado River is also high in salts. Leach out saline soils by applying water slowly for several hours to wash soil salts down and away from the plants' root zone. Some gardeners mix gypsum into the soil to alleviate the problem.

## Testing Soil

If plants have not grown properly around your home in the past and you think it could be a soil problem, have your soil tested. Most state cooperative extension services (California is an exception) perform soil testing. Private soil-testing labs will test your soil for a fee, or you can analyze your own soil with a test kit, available at nurseries. A soil analysis measures the pH—the acidity or alkalinity of the soil. Soil pH helps determine how nutrients are made available to plants, affecting their health and growth. The pH scale ranges from 3.5 (the most acid) to 9.5 (the most alkaline); 7 is neutral. Soils in the arid West tend to be more alkaline; soils in the eastern U.S. are more on the acid side. Most wildflowers prefer soil that is slightly acid to slightly alkaline, with a few exceptions.

## Improving Soils

It's generally a good idea to improve your soil if any of these conditions apply:

- Your soil is slow draining. A slow-draining soil *must* be improved if you are to successfully grow the majority of wildflowers.

- You are growing long-lived perennial wildflowers that will be in place for a number of years.

- Weed growth has not been a major problem in the past in the proposed planting sites.

- You are planting a small area where weeds can be controlled.

- Your goal is a highly attractive and densely planted garden appearance.

If soil improvement is on the agenda, the time to do it is before planting. Note: Extensive digging and mixing the soil often bring buried weed seeds to the surface where they can germinate. Be aware that if weeds were a problem in the past, soil preparation will probably aggravate it.

The easiest way to improve a hard-to-work, slow-draining soil is by adding organic matter. Well-aged animal manures, leaf mold, ground bark products and home-made compost are common amendments. To work a planting bed to a depth of about 6 inches, add a layer of organic matter about 2 inches deep over the area. Dig thoroughly into existing soil, blending it so there are no streaks or layers of material. Avoid an abrupt "begin and end" situation from improved soil to native soil. The soils should make a gradual transition from one to another so plant roots won't "stop" when the soil composition changes.

Organic matter mixed into sandy soils increases the nutrient- and water-holding capacity. It also improves the drainage and workability of heavy clay soils.

**Soil on slopes and hillsides**—These situations require special preparation to prevent soil erosion and to provide the proper environment to nurture seedlings. It sometimes helps to till the soil before applying water to allow penetration. When soil is ready to work, cultivate by tilling, disking or spading to 6 inches deep, then drag or

When planting individual plants in slow-draining hardpan or caliche soil, make a "chimney" to well-draining soil below.

Organic material mixed into the top 6 inches of soil improves drainage as well as the soil's ability to hold moisture and nutrients in the root zone.

Till proposed planting area, and water regularly to encourage weed seeds to germinate.

Allow weeds to grow until they become young seedlings.

Remove weeds with hoe, or better yet, by hand, disturbing the upper layer of soil as little as possible.

rake to create a seedbed. Leave the surface roughly cultivated so there are ridges. This will reduce erosion and create depressions for seeds to lodge where they'll receive more moisture and protection.

## Planting in Unimproved Soil

Leaving your soil as is and not adding amendments is recommended in certain circumstances. For example, it may not be practical to improve the soil for a large planting, such as a meadow. When the soil is left undisturbed, fewer dormant weed seeds are brought to the soil surface to germinate. If your soil is native and has not been moved around to aid your home's construction, it is probably well suited to grow the wildflowers native to your region. If this is the case, follow the steps listed below for Minor Weed Invasions.

# Weed Control

Keeping weed growth under control creates a less competitive environment for wildflower seedlings and mature plants. Because weeds are prolific producers of seed, with people, animals, birds and wind aiding in their distribution, controlling them requires continual attention. If the weeds and their seedheads are not removed from your plot of ground, the cycle of heavy annual weed growth will continue.

Control weeds before you plant to *prevent* them from getting a foothold. If you can, prepare or treat planting areas (see following) several months prior to planting. Treat in early summer for a fall planting and in early winter to plant in spring. When weeds do appear in newly planted wildflower plots, remove them when they are young, before seeds form, and when they are easier to pull from the soil. One of the best times for a weeding session is after an irrigation or rain. Tip: Become familiar with what weed seedlings look like, so you can tell them from your wildflower seedlings.

Avoid planting your wildflowers in areas where weeds have flourished in the past. Low-grade sites where rainwater accumulates are often weedy, and the soil will hold hundreds of seeds. Ideally, select a location that is at a higher grade with well-draining

soil. It will be less likely to harbor weed seeds.

## Control for Major Weed Invasions

This method should be used if weeds are a serious problem in the proposed planting site. It works on the principle that you rid the planting area of weeds by encouraging them to germinate and grow so you can kill them all at once.

Apply water to the future planting site a day or two before your assault. Moisture should reach about 8 inches deep. Using a shovel or rototiller, dig down 4 to 6 inches, turning the soil over. Grade and level the seedbed. Now wait and watch the weeds grow. Continue light applications of water for about 6 weeks, allowing weeds to develop into young seedlings. The rate of growth depends on temperature and day length. After weed growth is substantial, remove them with a hoe rake or (the best way) by pulling.

After the cycle of weed growth has been removed, till the soil again and allow weeds to grow, then remove them again. Your goal is to "get the weeds out of the system." It can take two or even three sessions until weed growth has reached a tolerable level.

One alternative to tedious hand-pulling of weeds is a process called *solarization*, where you "cook" the weeds with heat. Till and water the area as above, then cover the area with clear plastic (4 mils thick). Seal the perimeter with rocks or soil to hold in the heat, creating a greenhouse effect. Leave the plastic cover in place for four weeks, keeping the perimeter secure. The sun's heat will kill weeds and weed seeds near the soil surface. In most areas of the West, sunshine is plentiful, but if you live along the coast, fog and cloudy days during late spring and summer can affect the process. Plan ahead so the weather will likely be sunny to do a better job.

## Control for Minor Weed Invasions

This method goes hand in hand with planting wildflowers in unprepared soil. It works on the principle that the soil is disturbed as little as possible so weed seeds remain buried below the soil surface. This is also the best method for planting large areas where soil preparation is not practical or economical. If you use this method, perform the drainage test as described at the bottom of page 119 to be sure soil drainage is adequate.

Do not rake or dig the soil, but remove weeds, large rocks and debris in the area to be planted. Remove weeds as they appear, pulling by hand. After the site has been cleared, water thoroughly so moisture reaches to 8 inches deep. Wait until soil is moist but not soggy. Lightly cultivate soil, digging just an inch or two deep. The goal is to loosen the soil to create a seedbed that will improve germination. Sow seed according to instructions on page 118.

# Starting with Seed

Most wildflowers are easy to start from seed and are sown directly where you want plants to grow. For many wildflowers it is the best way because their shallow, fragile root systems are difficult to transplant. The selection of species available as seed is very extensive, much greater than what is available in containers at the nursery, although this is gradually changing. Addresses of mail-order seed suppliers are listed on page 111.

Most wildflowers prefer a sunny location that receives at least eight hours of sun each day, but some are adapted to grow better with some shade. Be aware, too, that in the hottest inland valleys and desert regions, afternoon shade is usually beneficial. And flowers don't fade as quickly with some shade. The information in the outside columns in the Gallery of Wildflowers, pages 37 to 110, gives the preferred exposures of each wildflower species.

## Wildflower Seed Mixes

In recent years, wildflower mixtures have been used as landscaping experiments of sorts by state highway and parks departments. Plantings were found to reduce grounds maintenance and create more colorful views. Likewise, golf courses increasingly include less water-demanding wildflowers to reduce maintenance while adding color and interest along the fairways and in the rough.

As a result of these large-scale practical applications, many wild-flower mixes are now available for home gardeners, with formulated blends of species appropriate for various climates and uses. Seed companies in North America generally offer seed mixes for eight or more general climate zones. Those most commonly represented include: the Northeast, Mideast, Southeast, Rocky Mountains, Texas, Southwest, California and the Northwest. For specific garden situations there are mixes for a cottage garden, dry locations, cutting garden, patio garden and dried flower garden.

These formulated mixes include species adaptable to designated zones. One of the rewards of planting a wildflower mix is the element of surprise as to which flower species emerge and develop. A seed mixture for a given climate zone generally includes 15 to 25 species of annuals and perennials with native and naturalized selections.

When you select a regional wildflower mix, it is important to consider your climate, particularly the amount of rainfall or availability of water required to establish a planting. From the moment seeds are planted and until seedlings reach a stage of being established, it is necessary to provide supplemental water. If you live in an area that receives 20 inches of rain, longer-lived perennial species should predominate. Some annual species should be included, however, to provide color the first season after planting. In contrast, in most dry regions—where rainfall is less than 15 inches a year—a higher percentage of annuals should make up the mix. No matter what the case, select a regional mix that most closely relates to the region where you live and garden. The more regional the mix, the better.

## How Much Seed to Sow?

Application rates for areas ranging from small, 100-square-foot gardens to acreage plantings are also provided for each wildflower in the Gallery descriptions. These are approximate amounts, calculated to create a solid stand when plants are mature. If you combine species to create your own wildflower mix, reduce the application rate of each species proportionately according to the number of species planted. If planting two species, reduce

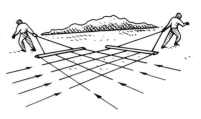

Mark and measure the area to be planted. A measuring board can be made by hammering nails in a board at equally spaced intervals. Drag over the prepared area. The lines left behind can serve as a guide to seeding coverage.

Many lawn fertilizer spreaders can be used to apply seed to large planting areas. Hand-held "whirlybird" type spreaders also work well.

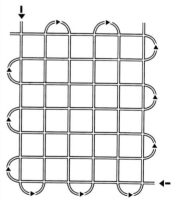

To ensure more even coverage, divide the amount of seed to be applied into two batches. Apply one batch of seed going north and south. Apply the second batch perpendicular to the first, going east and west.

Divide seed to be applied into two batches and apply as described on page 117 (bottom drawing). Use a broad sweeping motion to cast seed onto soil. Mixing soil with sand will make it easier to see where seed is applied.

Rake or press seed into soil. Double rake to ensure good seed-to-soil contact but don't bury seed too deep.

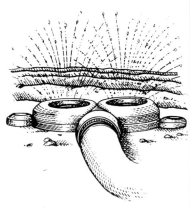

Apply water using a sprinkler that delivers a fine mist spray. If water puddles or washes the soil, the seed and resulting plant coverage will be uneven.

the amount by half. If planting four species, reduce to one-quarter, and so on.

Your soil type, available moisture, exposure to sun, planting season, hot and cold temperatures and amount of competition from weeds are some of the factors that affect how your wildflowers germinate and establish. As you gain experience and note how your favorite wildflowers perform, you'll be a better judge of the right amount of seed to plant (and when to plant) to obtain the results you want. Don't be afraid to experiment. Keeping a record of planting dates, seed amounts, germination times and methods of weed control will be invaluable as you expand the scope of your wildflower gardening.

## Pretreating Seeds to Increase Germination

Some plants have evolved natural defenses to help ensure their survival in the inhospitable conditions they face in the arid West. Chemical inhibitors and other mechanisms such as tough seed coats prevent seeds from germinating until certain conditions are met. In nature, these conditions are supplied by chance, such as roughing of the seed coat as it is washed headlong down a streambed after a violent summer storm, or being passed through a bird's digestive system. Others include an elaborate sequence of selected amounts of rainfall or cold temperatures. The fact is, wildflower seed germination is still much of a mystery. Little research has been performed to supply the right answers. Most of the information that is available is the result of trial and error by dedicated gardeners. Where pretreatment of seeds is known to increase germination, it is noted in the descriptions. Here are brief explanations of the most-common processes.

*Scarification* is a method in which the seed coat is softened or scratched to improve germination. Seed coats can be notched with a file or scratched by rubbing seeds between two sheets of medium sandpaper. Don't overdo it or the seed embryo will be damaged.

*Hot-water treatment*, soaking seeds in hot water, softens hard seedcoats and leaches away chemical inhibitors. Because small seeds are difficult to

scarify by mechanical means, this is the recommended method. Boil water and remove from heat. Add seeds, being sure water has ceased boiling to avoid damaging seed. Soak until seeds swell, after which they should be planted. In general, do not soak seed for more than 24 hours.

*Stratification* is a means of providing moist, cold temperatures prior to seeding, "fooling" the seed by signaling that conditions are correct and it is safe to germinate. Store seed in moist vermiculite (available at nurseries) in plastic bags and place in the refrigerator. Times for stratification vary from a few weeks to months, according to the plant. Check often to see if seeds have germinated and to be sure they are not moldy. Seeds that benefit from stratification are noted in the Gallery descriptions.

## Seed-Sowing Methods

When planting wildflowers in a small area, use the hand-seeding method, shown in the illustrations at left. Because most seed is quite small, it can be difficult to see where seed has been broadcast. Add sand to your seed mix so it is easier to see where seed is being applied. Mix one part of your seed mix thoroughly with three parts of white sand. If you have qualms about seeding properly by hand, practice with sand in another area until you feel confident you are applying the seed evenly.

If you are sowing seed over a large area, consider using a mechanical seed spreader. Certain brands of fertilizer spreaders can also double as seed applicators. It's helpful to mark out an evenly spaced grid over the planting area. These individual units of measurement will help you apply seed more evenly. Some gardeners also mark out seeding patterns with gypsum. Lightly spray the area to be seeded with water just before planting to darken the soil color. The application of the sand-and-seed mix will be more visible on the dark soil.

*Hydromulching* is one method of applying wildflower seeds in large areas and to sloping sites. It is done by commercial landscape firms, which use specialized tank trucks with high-pressure hoses to spray wildflower seed, water and paper mulch slurry directly onto the slope. It is recommended that the seed *not* be mixed with the slurry. (When the seed and slurry mix dries, it tends to pull away from the soil, leaving the seeds high and dry.) Rather, apply seed to the area, then follow with the slurry to hold seed in place and assist with germination.

**Seed-Sowing Tips**—Sow seed on a windless day. Use a broad, sweeping motion of the arm so seed will flow out in a graceful arc. To help ensure more even coverage, *double-sow* seed. Divide the quantity of seed to be planted in half. Use one half to make a pass going north and south. Use the second half and apply it going east and west.

The depth to plant seed varies according to wildflower species, but most wildflower seed is sown on the soil surface or planted shallowly—no deeper than 1/16 inch. One of the most common reasons for failure is planting seed too deep. One way to avoid deep planting is to sow seed on the soil and press into the surface to make good contact. If seed should be planted a bit deeper, lightly rake it into the soil, double raking much as in the seed-sowing method described above. Apply a thin layer of light organic mulch (be sure it is free of weed seeds) on the soil surface, if desired, to help retain soil moisture. Don't apply a thick layer of mulch or the germinating wildflower seeds might use all their energy before reaching the surface.

Water the seeded area directly after sowing with a sprinkler that emits a fine spray pattern. Water gently. Avoid puddling to prevent erosion and washing of the soil, which will also wash seeds away. Follow the watering program described on pages 120 to 122.

Germination periods for plants vary greatly, from one week to several weeks. Even with adequate moisture, many seeds of various species require longer periods than others to germinate, depending on hardness of the seed coat or the relationship between soil temperature and moisture. Generally, the warmer the soil temperature, the faster seeds will germinate, but even this is not true for all wildflowers.

## Thinning Plants

Do not allow all seedlings to grow. There won't be enough space for all of them to obtain proper amounts of moisture and nutrients and the entire stand will suffer. Thin seedlings when they reach 2 to 3 inches high. Tweezers that have a broad blade work well. Some gardeners use small children's scissors to trim away extra plants. Refer to the mature widths of plants in the Gallery descriptions for a guide to spacing.

# Starting with Container Plants

Container plants available at nurseries allow you to launch directly into the planting season. You can see what the plant looks like, and the effect can be almost instant. Perennial wildflowers are good candidates for container planting, since it can take two years or longer for them to reach flowering stage when started from seed. Container plants are more expensive, and often the selection is limited—most wildflowers are available only as seed. But more nurseries are offering a greater selection of wildflowers ready to plant from containers.

When nursery shopping, be aware that many native and adapted low-water plants look deceptively scrawny in their containers. Don't judge their potential by a few stems and leaves of immature plants, but do be selective. Avoid plants that are rootbound, with roots extending out the container bottom. Ideally, plants should have a robust, healthy appearance. Select a small plant with vigor rather than a larger, less robust specimen.

## Planting Container Plants, Step by Step

Plant on a cool, cloudy day. If you must plant on a sunny day, do it late in the afternoon. Preparing planting holes beforehand allows you to moisten soil deeply, providing a reservoir of moisture in the soil. Grade of planting beds should be located about 2 inches below surrounding paving or other hardscape.

Dig a hole as deep and as wide as the rootball. Loosen soil at bottom. Add water to the hole a day or two before planting. Test for drainage. Fill with water and allow to drain. Fill again. Water should drain in about three to four hours. If it hasn't, try another site

Water plant a few hours or so before planting. To remove plant, turn upside down and gently tap bottom of pot.

Dig a hole about twice as wide and as deep as the rootball. Plant should be situated in the ground at the same depth as it was in its container.

Fill soil in around rootball and firm gently around roots. Water well. See Watering, page 120, for a schedule on watering new plants.

Newly planted plants should have regular water applied to their root zone for several weeks after planting. In hottest regions, you may have to water twice a day, even more often when windy.

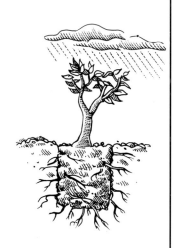

In most of the arid West, fall is the best time to plant. Air temperatures are moderate and soil temperatures are warm, promoting germination of seeds and root growth of container plants. Winter rains help get plants off to a good start the following spring.

or create a drainage chimney. For mass plantings, a power auger can be used to create multiple drainage channels. See the illustration on page 115.

Remove plant gently from pot. If soil mass is rootbound, use a knife or pruning shears to slice the outside of the rootball and gently splay it open. Set in planting hole and add in soil around the rootball, gently pressing soil around rootball. Water thoroughly to settle, and check planting depth of rootball. It should be the same as it was in its container. Build a soil basin to hold the water. Make it a few inches high and extend it just beyond the outer edge of the rootball. Be prepared to expand the basin as the plant grows.

Space plants far enough apart to allow them to develop to their mature size. See the Gallery of Wildflowers descriptions for mature heights and widths. If you combine annuals with perennials, be aware that annuals are often more vigorous growers, particularly during spring to early summer. They can crowd and retard the growth of slower-developing perennials. Keep annuals at least 18 inches away from crowns of perennials.

If temperatures are warm, shade newly planted plants from the afternoon sun. Use evergreen branches, palm fronds, baskets or boards stuck in the soil. Keep soil moist around the rootballs of new plantings for several weeks, gradually tapering off watering to follow a water-efficient irrigation program, described on page 122.

## When to Plant

In milder climates of the arid West, the fall season is the preferred planting time for spring-flowering wildflowers. During fall the soil is still warm. This helps promote improved germination of seeds and encourages root growth of plants set out from containers. At the same time, the air temperature is moderate, reducing evaporation of soil moisture at a time when regular moisture is crucial to seed and plant development. When weather conditions are milder than during the hot summer or cold winter months, plants have to endure less stress, so it is easier for them to become established. And, if the weather gods are willing, the gentle fall and winter rains nourish plants, reducing irrigation. As fall

progresses into winter and spring, the new seedlings and young plants are well rooted and quick to respond to the warmer weather of spring, producing healthy top growth and flowers.

In cold-winter regions, spring is the best planting period. Plant in spring after danger of frost has passed. In moderate coastal climates, planting can be done year-round, but more water is required to establish plants set out during late spring to summer due to the warmer temperatures.

## Watering

Premoisten the soil to 1 to 2 feet deep *before* seeding or planting. This provides a reservoir of moisture for developing plants. After seeding, apply water gently to prevent puddling and washing the tiny seeds out of the soil. Use a hose-end nozzle that has an adjustable spray or a fan spray to hand-water small areas. For large areas use a sprinkler on a base that can be moved easily.

Schedule a daily light sprinkling for newly seeded areas. Continue until seeds have sprouted and show three or four leaves. However, if the weather is cool or cloudy, skip a day or two. If it is windy, the upper 1 to 2 inches of soil can dry quickly, which may necessitate more frequent watering.

If plants are located on slopes, apply water in intervals. This helps prevent washing of seed, mulch and soil. Do this by watering for a determined period, such as 5 minutes, allowing water to soak into soil. Repeat later with another 5-minute watering, and so on, until the soil receives enough moisture.

After new plants show growth, gradually space out waterings, perhaps to two to three applications per week. After young plants reach the ready-to-flower stage, provide deep-penetrating irrigation about once every week or so. Water in the early morning when conditions are still and there is less evaporation. Morning watering also reduces the chance of root rot disease, which is prone to attack selected wildflower species.

Irrigations will be fewer along coastal areas and more frequent in the hot deserts and inland valleys. The amount of rainfall you receive in a given year also affects your watering schedule. If heat increases to 85F or more, or if winds are excessive, check each day for moisture in the top several inches of soil. Water if soil is dry. The top 4 to 6 inches of soil surface should be kept moist, but do not allow it to remain saturated at any time, which can suffocate plant roots.

## Watering Established Plants

As just discussed, newly planted container plants or seed-sown seedlings require moist (not wet) soil the first several weeks. Any dry period prevents roots from developing deeply and uniformly, and plant growth and appearance can be permanently affected. Adding a layer of organic mulch on the soil surface helps reduce evaporation of moisture from the soil.

Annual wildflowers are considered established when seedlings have made substantial growth to support 6 to 8 sets of leaves and they have begun to branch out. Perennial wildflowers are considered established after they have lived through a complete summer season.

To develop a watering program for established plants, understand the distinction between *duration* and *frequency*. Controlling the duration, how long each irrigation lasts, is important, because a long, slow irrigation allows water to soak the entire root zone. Frequency, how often you water, varies according to the age of the plant, exposure, time of year, the extent of the root zone and soil type. The more shallow the root system (as with new plants), the more frequent the irrigation. As your wildflowers become established, gradually *reduce* the frequency and *increase* the duration of irrigations. This will develop deeper root systems. Note that it is not as important to continue irrigations with annual wildflowers after they have reached peak flowering. Perennial wildflowers do require a more conscientious program to maintain health and vigor.

It helps to know when your plants show the first signs of stress so you can quickly adjust watering schedules to prevent loss of growth, injury or even death. Here are some key points to help you water plants efficiently.

**Know Your Soil Type**—Soil type affects the depth to which water goes into the soil, how quickly it gets into the root zone and how long it remains there. Most plants, but particularly those native to arid climates, require good soil drainage. Generally speaking, 1 inch of rain or irrigation in a sandy soil will go about 12 inches deep. For water to reach 3 feet deep, you'll need to apply water slowly for about 1-1/2 hours without runoff. Clay soils are dense and compact; one inch of water penetrates to only 4 or 5 inches. For water to reach 3 feet, you'll need to irrigate for about 4 hours. Loam soils, depending on the organic matter content, fall somewhere between these two extremes.

**Check for Soil Moisture**—The depth of water penetration in your soil will help guide your watering schedule. Dig down after an irrigation to see how far moisture has penetrated. Or push a long steel rod or screwdriver into irrigated soil. The rod stops penetrating when it reaches dry soil. A tool called a *soil sampler* will pull a narrow core of soil from the ground, showing the depth that moisture has penetrated. Doing this lets you see that the soil is dry and plants need a drink—*before* they become water-stressed.

**Know When Plants Show Signs of Water Need**—Plants show water need when leaf color turns from shiny to dull. Bright green leaves turn to blue or gray-green. Leaf tips and twigs turn brown. Drastic signs are new plant growth wilting or drooping, leaves curling and flowers fading quickly and dropping prematurely. Older leaves turn brown and dry and fall off.

**Encourage Deep Rooting with Deep Watering**—The depth to water depends on the plant. Roots of flowers such as annuals and some perennials reach 1 to 1-1/2 feet, small shrubs down to 3 feet. Tree roots reach to 5 feet or much more, depending on the species. Plant roots that go deep in the soil are better insulated against heat and cold, are anchored better against winds and have a greater reservoir from which to draw water when it is not provided on a regular basis. Shallow-rooted plants have none of these advantages. The upper soil layers dry out quickly, and the first strong wind can knock plants over. Deep

Shallow watering, sprinkling the soil, causes plants to produce shallow roots. The upper layer of soil dry out quickly and plants tend to suffer from stress.

Deep watering helps produce deep roots. Plants have a greater reservoir of moisture to draw upon, and are insulated from hot or cold temperatures near the soil surface.

To maintain a planting's natural appearance yet control height, selectively *thin* vertical branches, making pruning cuts close to a lateral stem or branch.

To control plant width, cut side growth and lateral branches to upright-growing stems.

"Deadheading" blooms that are past their prime encourages plants to produce more flowers, and keeps them looking neat.

watering also washes damaging soil salts down and away from plant roots.

**Put Water Where It's Needed**—As plants grow, most roots grow and extend out and away from the plant. The roots that absorb water—the feeder roots—tend to be concentrated at the outside edges of (and beyond) the plant's *drip line*—the area where rainwater drips off leaves to the ground. Extend a shallow watering basin almost to the trunk and to just past the plant's canopy. This helps ensure that plant roots are getting the greatest benefit from the moisture you're supplying.

**Water When Evaporation Rates Are Low**—Wind movement across plants not only disperses water elsewhere, it increases transpiration by moving water vapor rapidly away from leaf surfaces. Low humidity also increases transpiration. In tandem with windy weather, it can cause extensive water loss. High heat such as that at midday during summer increases loss due to evaporation. Water during the cool times of day—evening or early morning—when there is little or no wind.

**Install Drip Irrigation**—A drip irrigation system can be used to irrigate wildflowers in certain situations. It can be used to water narrow beds or garden-setting plantings of wildflowers. Low-flow irrigation *fan jets* are recommended; they apply water as a fine spray to small-scale mass plantings (4 to 8 feet in diameter). Use *emitters* to apply water to the root zone of larger perennials and to container plants. Drip is not recommended for large meadows.

## Fertilizing

For the most part, wildflowers do not require fertilizer to stay healthy. They actually grow better without it. Fast-acting chemical or liquid fertilizers in particular encourage rapid, excessive, soft, sprawling growth that is more susceptible to disease and insect attack. Note, however, that wildflowers in an intensely planted situation such as a garden border are more apt to need additional nutrients.

Some soils may be lacking the basic nutrients—nitrogen, phosphorus and potassium—required for plant growth. Nitrogen is the nutrient that is usually lacking. Plants use a lot of nitrogen and it is leached out of the root zone, particularly in sandy soils. Phosphorus is often lacking in clay soils. It does not "move" in the soil, so it should be worked in before planting where it can be absorbed by the roots. Potassium is generally in good supply.

If plants show signs of poor growth, apply compost or fertilizer. Use approximately one-third of the amount recommended on the label. If plants appear to be lacking in nutrients, showing poor color and growth, apply a diluted liquid fertilizer and water in thoroughly.

Cold-hardy perennial wildflowers can be fed twice a year—early in spring just prior to new growth and again in early summer. Water fertilizer in immediately after applying, and wash it off leaves. Applying compost as a mulch and digging it into the soil around plants will also supply some nutrients to plants. Organic fertilizers such as cottonseed meal, composted manure and slow-release fertilizers are less likely to overfertilize or burn plants.

## Maintenance

When plants are midway through their growth cycle, there might be a need to control growth. If your goal is a natural garden appearance, do not shear plants. Rather, selectively thin excess interior growth and wayward branches. Make all pruning cuts close to stems or branches, leaving no stubby leftovers. This helps maintain the plant's natural form while controlling its growth. Do not remove growth at the base of plants so that trunks or main stems are bare. Allow branches to drape and trail to the ground. To reduce a plant's height, cut vertical growth down to and flush with a laterally growing stem or branch. To reduce a plant's width, cut side growth and lateral branches to upright-growing stems.

*Deadheading* is the simple process of removing flowerheads that are well past their prime. This keeps plants looking fresh, and the plant's energy goes into flower production that would otherwise be used to produce seed. Many gardeners deadhead their perennial and wildflower plantings as a matter of routine, inspecting the garden every few days. Flowers with long stems should have the stems removed as well to maintain the plant's appearance. Plants that produce flower spikes, such as *Penstemon* and *Salvia,* should be cut back to the first set of leaves. This often causes the plant to produce a new wave of flowers.

Some perennial wildflowers can be reduced by as much as one-third after bloom to encourage plants to bloom again later in the season or produce vigorous new growth for more flowers the following season. Use pruning shears to make cuts close to the remaining branch or stem. Make major cuts first to maintain the plant structure and form.

Winter-dormant perennials such as *Rudbeckia* and *Helianthus* can be pruned back close to the plant's basal growth at the end of the season—late fall or early winter. New growth will emerge the following spring. If plants are damaged by frost, wait until spring and remove dead wood after new growth begins.

**Staking**—Some large-growing wildflowers, especially those that produce profuse numbers of flowers, such as cosmos, cannot stand up to wind and rain on their own and sprawl all over the planting area. Providing stakes or other supports keeps plants upright, in control and looking attractive. Staking must be done early, before the plant shows signs of needing support, or the stalk or clump will be damaged by the next strong wind or rain. Staking early allows the plant to grow around the support and mask it with leaves. The underpinning should not be visible. The type of support used depends on the plant. The illustrations at right show two simple methods of staking plants for protection.

Some perennials, such as *Rudbeckia* species, grow rapidly and tend to sprawl as the bloom period approaches. To prevent, nip the growing tips of branches to produce side growth and strengthen the main stems. If the plants do sprawl, cut back the arching stems. You'll get control and the selective pruning will produce new flowering stems.

## Mulches

A mulch is a layer of material, often organic, that is used to cover the bare soil around plants. A mulch has many beneficial uses: It helps control weeds that compete for moisture and nutrients. Cultivation of the soil is reduced so that few weed seeds are brought to the soil surface. (The weeds that do grow up through a mulch are easier to remove than those rooted in soil.) Mulches slow evaporation of soil moisture. For example, a thin layer of mulch applied over newly seeded areas helps keep moisture in the upper layer of soil for a longer period of time, assisting germination. Mulches moderate soil temperatures, cooling the upper layers of soil where plant roots are located. This is especially helpful during summer. Mulches also spruce up the look of things and add organic matter to the soil as they decay.

Leaf mold, shredded leaves, straw, compost, pine needles, grass clippings and ground bark are common organic mulches. The region where you live will determine to a certain extent which materials are generally available. Inorganic mulches such as rock, pea gravel and decomposed granite also conserve moisture and reduce weeds, but they do not break down to improve the soil. They are often used as a ground cover around flowering plants in place of lawn or living ground cover.

In mild-winter areas, add a layer of mulch over the plant root zone *after* temperatures warm in spring. This allows the soil to warm, which encourages plant growth. Apply before heat gets intense to reduce moisture loss through evaporation and to modify the soil temperature.

## End-of-the-Season Cleanup

Annual and perennial native wildflowers have the ability to regrow and bloom year after year once established. Annuals regrow from seed produced by the original plantings. Perennials also produce seed and regrow from their roots the following year to produce new, fresh growth. With proper care, wildflower plantings gradually improve in appearance as the plants take hold and become more established.

To protect tall, columnar plants from breaking in the wind, support with one stake and tie stalks in two or three places. Use soft cloth, soft twine or twist-tie.

Pruned branches from trees or shrubs can be pushed into ground to become natural supports for tall-growing plants. With time, wildflower growth will conceal the branches.

One of the benefits of applying a mulch around plants is that weeds can be removed much easier. The best time to do this is after rainfall or irrigation.

When the bloom season is over and plants have declined, cut back stems and branches to 4 to 6 inches high and remove the dead growth. This cleans up the area and helps dispurse seeds for the following year.

Shake all branches or stems that hold seedheads to scatter seeds where you want new plants to grow.

**Naturalizing a Wildflower Planting—** To cause your wildflowers to reseed in place, wait until all flowering has ceased and seeds have formed. (See Collecting Seed, following.) This generally takes two to three weeks after the last flowers have bloomed and plant stems have turned brown. Cease watering. Use a nylon line trimmer or hedge clippers to cut all stems and branches to 4 to 6 inches high. (If you cut much lower it can damage or destroy perennial species.) Make a couple of passes to ensure that the stems, leaves and seeds are thoroughly chopped and scattered over the planting area. It may be necessary to pass a power mower set at the highest level over the plant materials to chop them thoroughly. Rake and remove the dead stems and leaves, shaking them to disperse any seeds that might cling to the stems. Be aware that some wildflowers (those with succulent stems) seem to disappear after plants decline, leaving few stems or leaves to clean up. These include California poppy, California bluebells and owl's clover.

If your area will be irrigated during summer, be prepared to reseed most annual wildflowers in fall to renew the planting. Many native annuals require a dry summer period, and the summer irrigation and soil moisture cause the seeds to rot and die. This is particularly true in California's Mediterranean climate.

**Collecting Seed—**If you want to extend plantings to other parts of the garden or share seeds with friends and neighbors, collect a portion of your wildflower seeds before scattering them as described above. Check seed to see if it's ready to harvest. Most seeds change in color from green to brown, tan or black. Also, if seeds release easily from their pod or the pod has split, exposing seeds, they are generally ready to harvest. Remove as much of the stems, chaff and plant parts as possible to avoid contamination from insect larvae and disease. Place in a tight-fitting jar or plastic ziplock bag. Label with the seed type and date. Adding a small amount of silica gel will absorb moisture so seeds will not become moldy. Dry sand can serve as a substitute. Store in a cool, dry, dark location, such as the kitchen cupboard.

# Common Pests and Controls

Clean, healthy, strong-growing plants in well-draining soil seldom have serious problems with diseases or insects. In addition, a natural meadow or mixed wildflower border rarely suffers from pests or diseases due to the diversity of plant species. Natural garden designs also attract birds, lizards and predatory insects such as ladybugs and praying mantids that will help control harmful insects.

Occasionally, plants become susceptible to pests and diseases. This occurs more frequently when they are overfertilized or stressed by heat or drought. The following are some common pests to look out for.

**Insects and Related Pests—**Typical pests include aphids, spider mites, slugs, snails, blister beetles, caterpillars and leaf miners. Inspect plants every week or so, looking closely at undersides of leaves. Using a photographer's hand-held magnifying lens (10 to 14 power) is one way to identify insect pests as well as diseases.

Pests such as aphids and spider mites can be largely controlled by hosing them off with a strong stream of water. Some gardeners spray them with a dilute solution of dish soap, 1/5 cup to 1 gallon of water. Caterpillars and beetles can be removed by hand. Serious infestations of caterpillars and other larvae can be controlled by using Bacillus thuringiensis (Bt). This is a biological control that introduces a disease into the insect.

**Animal Pests—**Birds, rabbits, gophers, ground squirrels, moles and deer may find your wildflower plants a nice addition to their diets. To protect valuable, container-planted plants from gophers, line the planting hole with chicken wire to protect the root area. Sturdy fencing will help keep rabbits and squirrels from getting to your plants, but the animals are highly resourceful so don't depend on it. Individual cages around the most desirable plants may be necessary until they can get big enough to withstand a browsing. It may be necessary to stretch plastic netting or chicken wire over freshly sown plots to protect the seeds and young seedlings from birds.

# Public Gardens to Visit

Public botanical gardens and arboretums are excellent places to visit and learn about the wildflowers and native plants adapted to your region. Contact the gardens listed here for more detailed information on the plants and gardens featured, as well as best times of year to see gardens and plant displays.

## ARIZONA GARDENS

Desert Botanical Garden
1201 North Galvin Parkway
Phoenix, AZ 85008
(602) 941-1225
(602) 481-8131 Wildflower
Hotline March through April.
145 acres of landscaped grounds of desert-adapted plants.

Boyce Thompson Southwestern Arboretum
37615 Highway 60
Superior, AZ 85273
(520) 689-2811
Over 35 acres and two miles of nature trails through desert gardens and plants.

Tohono Chul Park
Exhibit Hall, Gift Gallery and Tea Room
7366 North Paseo del Norte
Tucson, AZ 85704
(520) 575-8468 for recorded information
(520) 742-6455
Over 400 plant species on 48 acres of demonstration gardens and nature trails, including many patios, ramadas and special gardens.

Tucson Botanical Gardens
2150 North Alvernon Way
Tucson, AZ 85712
(520) 326-9686
Over 5 acres of gardens, including a wildflower garden and Xeriscape demonstration garden.

## CALIFORNIA GARDENS

Arboretum of Los Angeles County
301 North Baldwin Avenue
Arcadia, CA 91007-2697
(818) 821-3222 or (213) 821-3214
Over 127 acres of landscaped grounds and plant collections.

Univ. of California at Berkeley
Berkeley Botanical Garden
Centennial Drive at Strawberry Canyon
Berkeley, CA 94720
(510) 643-8040 or 642-3343 for recorded message
30 acres of gardens with over 12,000 plant species.

Rancho Santa Ana Botanic Garden
1500 North College Avenue
Claremont, CA 91711
(714) 625-8767
86 acres of native California plants, including more than 1,500 species.

Sherman Library and Gardens
2647 East Pacific Coast Hwy.
Corona del Mar, CA 92625
(714) 673-2261
Horticultural display gardens of hanging baskets, annuals and tropical and subtropical plants.

Davis Arboretum
Univ. of California at Davis
Davis, CA 95616
(916) 752-2498
Over 100 acres of gardens. Emphasis given to California native plants.

Quail Botanical Gardens
230 Quail Gardens Drive
Encinitas, CA 92024
(619) 436-3036
(619) 436-8301 Herbarium for plant information
Over 30 acres of landcaped grounds, with trails, gardens and pools.

Fullerton Arboretum
California State Univ., Fullerton
P. O. Box 34080
Fullerton, CA 92634-9480
(714) 773-3579

26 acres of gardens, with botanical collections from around the world.

Univ. of California at Irvine Arboretum
(North Campus)
Irvine, CA 92717
(714) 856-5833
10 acres of gardens, with emphasis on cacti and succulents, as well as flowering bulbs and corms.

Descanso Gardens
1418 Descanso Drive
La Canada, CA 91011
(818) 952-4400; (818) 952-4401
Over 165 acres, including a 15-acre California native plant garden.

The Hortense Miller Garden
Recreation and Social Services Department
505 Forest Avenue
City of Laguna Beach, CA 92651
(714) 497-0716 (Extension 3)
A 2-1/2-acre private residence, containing many surprises and over 100 plant species. Call ahead for reservations.

Antelope Valley California Poppy Reserve
15101 West Lancaster Road
Lancaster, CA 93536
(805) 942-0662 (office)
(805) 724-1180 (reserve)
Wildflower Hotline:
(805) 948-1322.
A 1,700-acre preserve of California poppies and other native wildflowers.

The Living Desert
47900 Portola Avenue
Palm Desert, CA 92260
(619) 346-5694
Over 1,200 acres, with 20 acres in natural desert gardens, live desert animals and demonstration gardens.

South Coast Botanical Garden
26300 Crenshaw Boulevard
Palos Verdes Peninsula, CA 90274
(310) 544-1847
Over 87 acres of gardens, demonstration plots and natural landscapes.

Landscapes Southern California Style
450 Alessandro Boulevard
Riverside, CA 92517
(909) 780-4170
A one-acre garden designed to teach ways to design and create colorful low-water gardens.

Univ. of California at Riverside Botanic Garden
UCR Campus
Riverside, CA 92521
(909) 787-4650 for recorded message
39 acres of natural gardens, with over 3,000 plants arranged by plant community.

Strybing Arboretum & Botanical Gardens
Golden Gate Park
Ninth Avenue at Lincoln Way
San Francisco, CA 94122
(415) 753-7089
75 acres within Golden Gate Park consisting of many specialty gardens and over 8,000 plant species.

The Huntington Library, Art Collections and Botanical Gardens
1151 Oxford Road
San Marino, CA 91108
(818) 405-2141
150 acres of gardens, organized by themes such as Desert, Japanese and Jungle. More than 14,000 plant species.

Santa Barbara Botanic Garden
1212 Mission Canyon Road
Santa Barbara, CA 93105
(805) 682-4726
65 acres of preserve and displays of California native plants.

Wrigley Memorial and Botanical Garden
1400 Avalon Canyon Road
PO Box 2739
Santa Catalina Island
Avalon, CA 90704
(310) 510-2288
3 acres of developed gardens on 38 acres, including cacti, succulents and plants native to the California islands.

The Theodore Payne Foundation for Wildflowers and Native Plants, Inc.
10459 Tuxford Street
Sun Valley, CA 91352
(818) 768-1802 for recorded message
(818) 768-3533 Wildflower Hotline from March to May
Over 21 acres of natural plantings of California natives and wildflowers, containing over 800 plant species. Includes a 3-acre Wildflower Hill.

Filoli
Canada Road
Woodside, CA 94602
(415) 364-2880
16 acres of gardens organized into four themes: Sunken Garden, Walled Garden, Woodland Garden and Panel Garden.

## COLORADO GARDENS

Denver Botanic Gardens
1005 York Street
Denver, CO 80206
(303) 331-4000
(303) 331-4010 for recorded information
(303) 370-8032 (TDD)
22 acres of gardens including a Plains Garden, Xeriscape Garden and Rock Alpine Garden.

Chatfield Arboretum
8500 Deer Creek Canyon Road
Littleton, CO 80123
(303) 973-3705
A 700-acre natural area. Includes grassland, wetland, and historic farmstead.

## IDAHO GARDENS

Sawtooth Community Garden Project
102 Gimlet Road
Ketchum, ID 83340
(208) 726-9358
Five acres of gardens, including passive solar greenhouse.

## NEVADA GARDENS

Ethel M Botanical Garden
2 Cactus Garden Drive
Henderson, NV 89014
(702) 458-8864
2 acres of desert shrubs, trees and cacti.

Las Vegas Desert Demonstration Gardens
3701 West Alta Drive
Las Vegas, NV 89153
(702) 258-3205
A small water-conservation garden, containing over 160 plant species.

Univ. of Nevada, Las Vegas Arboretum
Box 451013
4505 Maryland Parkway
Las Vegas, NV 89154
(702) 895-3392
An on-campus arboretum on the grounds of UNLV.

## NEW MEXICO GARDENS

Living Desert Zoo and Gardens State Park
1504 Skyline Drive
Carlsbad, NM 88220
(505) 887-5516
Mailing address
PO Box 100
Carlsbad, NM 88221
1,107 acres, of which 35 are developed. Animals and plants of the Chihuahuan Desert.

New Mexico State Univ. Botanical Garden
Department of Agronomy and Horticulture Box 3Q
Las Cruces, NM 88003-0003
(505) 646-3405
Over 2 acres of gardens and demonstration plots.

## TEXAS GARDENS

Austin Area Garden Center
(in Zilker Park)
2220 Barton Springs Road
Austin, TX 78746
(512) 477-8672
Includes several separate theme gardens, including Xeriscape Garden and Butterfly Garden.

National Wildflower Resource Center (NWRC)
4801 La Crosse Ave.
Austin, TX 78739
(512) 292-4100
(512) 292-4200 Wildflower bloom information.
60 acres, including greenhouses and research plots. An excellent source of information on native plants and their conservation.

Corpus Christi Botanical Gardens
8545 South Staples
Corpus Christi, TX 78413
(512) 852-2100
Native plant displays and nature walk.

Dallas Arboretum and Botanical Society
8617 Garland Road
Dallas, TX 75218
(214) 327-8263
66 acres, including 25 acres of landscaped gardens.

Dallas Horticulture Center
(in Fair Park)
3601 M.L.K. Blvd.
PO Box 152537
Dallas, TX 75315
(214) 428-7476
8 acres of gardens, including the Benny J. Simpson Texas Native Plant Collection.

Fort Worth Botanic Garden
3220 Botanic Garden Drive North
Fort Worth, TX 76107
(817) 871-7686
114 acres, including many specialty gardens.

Houston Arboretum and Nature Center
4501 Woodway Drive
Houston, TX 77024
(713) 681-8433
155 acres, 5 miles of trails, educational Discovery Room, herb garden, wildflower garden.

Mercer Arboretum and Botanic Gardens
22306 Aldine Westfield
Humble, TX 77338
(713) 443-8731
214 acres, including many specialty gardens.

Judge Roy Bean Visitor Center
Corner of Loop 25 and Torres Avenue
PO Box 160
Langtry, TX 78871
(915) 291-3340
2-acre cactus garden.

San Antonio Botanic Garden
555 Funston Place
San Antonio, TX 78209
(512) 821-5115 or 821-5143 for recorded information
30 acres of gardens, half of which are dedicated to showcasing native Texas plants.

## UTAH GARDENS

Utah Botanical Gardens
1817 North Main Street
Farmington, UT 84025
(801) 451-3204
7 acres of landscaped gardens, including an area devoted to native plants.

Red Butte Garden and Arboretum
Univ. of Utah
300 Wakara Way
Salt Lake City, UT 84108
(801) 581-5322
Over 300 species of trees located throughout the 1,500-acre campus.

# Index